Corporate Governance:
A Board Director's Pocket Guide 3rd Ed.

Leadership, Diligence, and Wisdom

Eric Yocam, DBA, MS

Annie Choi, JD, MIB

YOCAM PUBLISHING LLC

Washington

Printed in the United States of America
ISBN-10: 0996104704
ISBN-13: 978-0-9961047-0-8

DISCLOSURE

All references to people, places, publications, Web sites, institutions, and databases are strictly provided to the reader for informational purposes only. The authors and publisher of this publication neither endorse nor promote any of the references found in this publication over any other reference not represented in this publication.

CONTENTS

Part III
Governance Trends and Globalization

ACKNOWLEDGEMENT

A set of supportive family members, friends, and professional associates made the work on this publication both pleasant and productive. The authors wish to thank everyone for their patience, encouragement and continued support.

Preface

The *Corporate Governance: A Board Director's Pocket Guide (or simply Pocket Guide)* is a publication that takes the form of an easy to use guide book and was written by the authors with particular type of reader in mind including active board director, investor, instructor, student, governance practitioner, lawyer, international reader, and anyone interested in the subject of corporate governance. This is the third edition with a significant number of revisions to the previous material that helps to round out the publication. The revised *Pocket Guide* builds upon previous relevant content and contemporary thought in corporate governance. The *Pocket Guide* continues to be ideal for readers who are at every interest level and want to learn more about governance and specifically corporate governance. The *Pocket Guide* is also ideal for those who have limited time to condense the various aspects, insights, and perspectives on the subject of corporate governance.

Many publications have already been written on the subject of corporate governance yet authors continue to provide insights into this constantly evolving subject. A significant amount of foundational material must be understood prior to addressing the more complex subjects of corporate governance with the intent of the authors to present both foundational and an appreciation for the complexities of mastering the art of corporate governance. The *Pocket Guide* should not be considered an exhaustive tome of in-depth corporate governance subjects. The authors of the *Pocket Guide* attempt to summarize the key aspects and provide a practical source for a quick review by a busy person.

The *Pocket Guide* is organized in a convenient and easy-to-use guide covering numerous subjects in corporate governance. What sets the *Pocket Guide* apart from other lengthy manuals? Simply, an overriding goal for the authors of this *Pocket Guide* is to present the corporate governance principles in a brief yet complete and easy-to-use manner. The *Pocket Guide* incorporates a number of helpful features:

✓ **Handbook Format**	❖ To make information easy to find, the *Pocket Guide* presents major principles in each chapter as statements of key ideas.
✓ **Easy-to-use**	❖ The *Pocket Guide* presents clear explanations and provides a convenient resource for use by a leader, practitioner, scholar, and anyone interested in the subject of corporate governance.
✓ **Latest Research**	❖ Every effort is taken to ensure the content within the *Pocket Guide* is supported with the most recent research from a number of reliable public data sources.

The subjects in the *Pocket Guide* were chosen because they are considered key subjects for a reference guide of this nature. Bullets under each subject present the main points and can serve as a springboard to further research.

Part I
Governance Overview

Introduction

What's ahead of us?

President Obama on July 21, 2010 signed into law the Dodd-Frank Wall Street Reform and Consumer Protection Act. This acts key provisions include consumer and investor protection, executive compensation, "Say on pay" vote once every three years by shareholders, corporate governance proxy access, and reason for same person as both Chair and CEO. However, not in the Act are limits on executive compensation and majority voting for directors in board elections

Of Previous Concern

In the 2nd edition, the authors' focus was on the economic crisis starting in 2008 that is believed to have occurred because of global inflation, increased unemployment, high oil and food prices, a declining dollar value, a horrible housing market and a subprime mortgage crisis. A so called perfect storm of economic conditions has triggered an extraordinary downward spiral: the subprime meltdown, liquidity crisis, extreme market volatility, controversial government bailouts, consolidations of major banking institutions and widespread economic turmoil both domestically and abroad. Many corporations now find themselves in uncharted territory, with a new paradigm of unpredictability trumping formerly reasonable expectations. In the coming year, board of directors will need to respond to the challenges and pressures of this new environment.

What's behind us now?

- ➢ "Say on pay" policies would give shareholders a non-binding advisory vote on executive compensation.
- ➢ Activist shareholders (e.g. Carl Icahn) will continue their multi-pronged campaigns to shift decision-making power away from boards and thereby exacerbate pressures to enhance short-term performance.
- ➢ Complexity will continue to grow (companies have prioritized size-revenue growth specifically through acquisitions - and not the associated complexity that comes from such growth).
- ➢ Regulatory system will have to be changed.

Independence of Board Directors

➢ Our Courts have yet to rule on independence: either the independence of venture capitalists on private company boards or large investors on public company boards.
➢ Both groups are conflicted.

Previous Boardroom Issues

➢ Role of Boards and their partnership with management.
➢ Information, knowledge and a board members' understanding of the company.
➢ Risk Management.
➢ Board activities in relation to strategy and management succession.

Board directors can be compared to "part-time employees" in that they work 125 to 250 hours per year (on average), and thus do not have all of the information needed to do the job that they are either asked or required to do.

Since corporations require a governing board of directors two primary factors a key to shaping how effective they are. The factors are good leadership and sharing collective wisdom between board directors and management to improve managerial judgment. Additionally, a threat of shareholder litigation in state courts should translate into additional motivation for board directors to engage in active governance of the corporation.

Directors should focus on those eight areas that results in generating the most value including[1] 1) strategy, 2) risk management, 3) tone at the top, 4) measuring and monitoring performance, 5) transformational transactions, mergers, acquisitions, partnerships, joint ventures, 6) management evaluations, compensation, and succession planning, 7) external communications and 8) board dynamics.

A board director's accountability and due diligence in decision making requires the management team to achieve milestones for the goals and plans that the boards of directors establish. There should also be a realization that serving on a company's board of directors is a tremendous honor as well as a tremendous responsibility. There continues to be a growing concern about the effectiveness of a company's board of directors because the added time and attention that boards require does not necessarily translates into better governance or even governance that adds value to the business. Even under improved processes and structures, a board director cannot claim to have the capability to conduct meaningful assessments and testing in many circumstances; especially, the amount of legal compliance and the limited time to process all of the information generated from a company.

Corporate Governance in the Nineteenth Century

➤ Shareholders concern about administrative pay and stock losses lead to corporate governance reform.

➤ Most of the large publicly traded corporations in the United States are incorporated under Delaware law, which is known to be friendly for forming corporations.

➤ A trade-off between rights of corporate boards to govern without unanimous consent of shareholders and statutory benefits like appraisal rights enacted through enhancements made in state corporation law.

Corporate Governance in the Twentieth Century

➤ The managerial class expands after World War II as well as with the emergence of multinational corporations.

➤ Agency theory gains significant ground. This theory reflects the concern with the agency relationship in which one party (the principal) delegates work to another (the agent), who performs that work.[2]

➤ The Separation of Ownership and Control establishes agency theory as the foundation for understanding corporate governance where the company represents a series of contracts.[3]

➤ Nature of the Company introduces the notion of transaction costs into the reasoning behind formation of the corporation.

➤ The Modern Corporation and Private Property set the stage for conception of corporate governance.[4]

➤ Following the Wall Street Crash of 1929, legal scholars suggest changing role of the modern corporation in American society.

Perspectives about corporate governance vary, but most can be traced to the three following theories. Prospective board members should have a basic understanding of these three theories in the context of the purpose of a board and how well a governance body can govern.

Agency Theory

In agency theory and corporate governance, self-interested board directors appropriate value to themselves. Hence, conflict arises because the board director is acting as an agent on behalf of the shareholder. Agency theory is about resolving two problems that can occur in agency relationships.[5] For example, in the case of a board director, two agency problems exist. First, the desires or goals of the shareholder and board director are in conflict. Second, the oversight is both difficult and expensive for the shareholder to verify what the board director is actually doing on the shareholder's behalf.

Say on pay

The term "say on pay" is used for a rule in corporate law whereby a corporation's shareholders have the right to vote on the remuneration of board directors.

➤ Litigation initiated by shareholders has begun against companies including Apple Inc., Microsoft Corp., Brocade Communications Systems Inc. and Symantec Corp. for executive pay disclosure.[6]
➤ A corporation's board directors are likely to overpay themselves because, directly or indirectly, they are allowed to pay themselves as a matter of general management.
➤ Board directors are elected to a board that has a fiduciary duty to protect the interests of the corporation. For public corporations, executive compensation is usually determined by a compensation committee comprised of board members.
➤ The effect of 'say on pay' measures can be binding or non-binding, depending on regulatory requirements or internal corporate policy as determined by proxy votes.
➤ The United Kingdom was the forerunner in mandating that shareholders be allowed a non-binding, or advisory vote on pay.

> ➢ In the United Kingdom, S 439 of the Companies Act 2006 mandates a vote on board director pay at the yearly annual meeting.

Research suggests that when a leader is considering what constitutes shareholder value, a leader should also consider that, in practice, the value proposition might not hold up, given the gap between the stakeholder's expectation and the realities of fulfilling that expectation.[7]

Stakeholder Theory

Research suggests that in addition to stakeholder theory, the existence of a complex bargaining process involves multiple interests. Multiple (or competing) interests can be found at each level of management within a company, including the board of director.[8]

A stakeholder board may be less efficient at generating total benefits. The stakeholder theory defines different groups of interest.[9] They sometimes compete, but they desire the same end, that is, to receive some type of benefit.[10] The traditional perspective on corporate governance comes from both agency and stakeholder theories[11] (refer to figure 1).

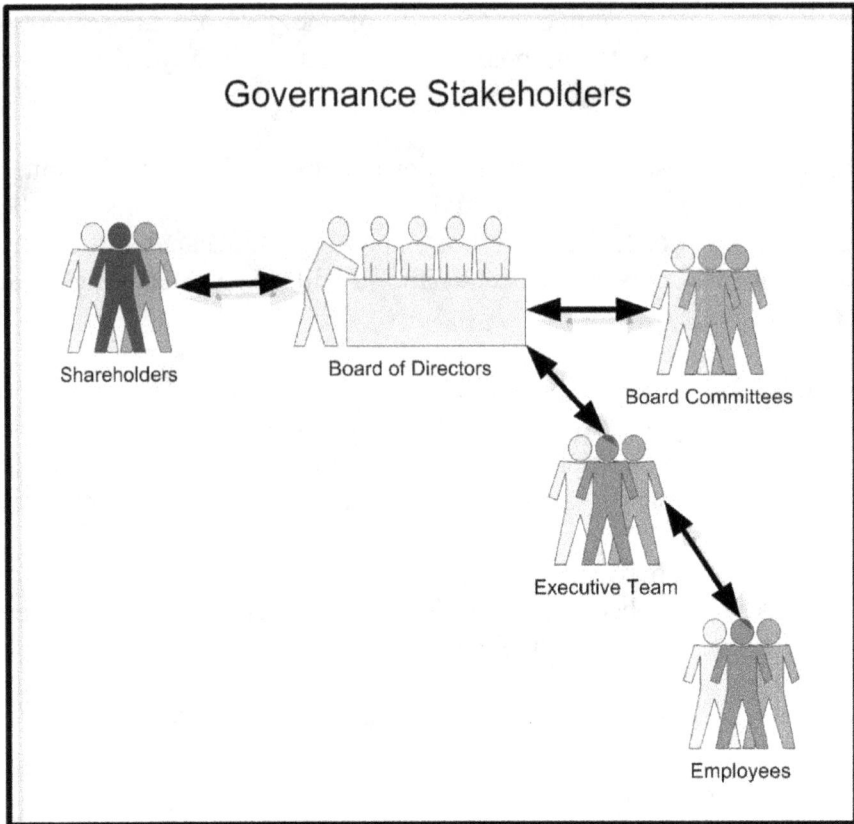

Figure 1 - Governance Stakeholders

Stewardship Theory

In stewardship theory of corporate governance, board directors maximize value for the company. In agency theory, the allocation of the board is by shareholders. In stewardship theory, the allocation of the board is by the managers. [12] Stewardship theory applied to corporate governance means that as an agent, on behalf of the stakeholder, a board director's motivation is to do a good job managing corporate assets because he or she is a good steward.

ENDNOTES

1. Salo (2013).
2. Eisenhardt (1989).
3. Fama and Jensen (1983).
4. Low (2006).
5. Elson and Ferrere (2013).
6. See "Suing about say on pay" (2013).
7. Chowdhury (2003), p. 140.
8. Morgan (1994).
9. Williamson and Bercovitz (1997).
10. Friedman and Miles (2002).
11. Caldwell and Ranjan (2005).
12. Turnbull (1997).

REFERENCES

Eisenhardt, K. (1989). Agency theory: An assessment and review. *Academy of Management Review*, 14(1), 57-74.

Elson, C. M., Ferrere, C. K. (2013). Surplus, agency theory, and the Hobbesian corporation. Wake Forest Law Review, 48(3), 721-744.

Fama, E. F., Jensen, M. C. (1983). Separation of ownership and control. *Journal of law and economics*, 301-325.

Caldwell, C., K. Ranjan. (2005). Organizational governance and ethical systems: A covenantal approach to building trust. *Journal of Business Ethics,* 2(58), 249–259.

Chowdhury, S. (2003). *Organization 21C: Someday all organizations will lead this way.* Upper Saddle River, N.J.: Prentice Hall.

Friedman, A., Miles, S. (2002). Developing Stakeholder Theory. *Journal of Management Studies*, 39(1), 1–21.

Low, C. (2006). A framework for the governance of social enterprise. *International journal of social economics*, *33*(5/6), 376-385.

Morgan, T. (1994). *Untying the knot of war: A bargaining theory of international crises.* Ann Arbor: University of Michigan Press.

Salo, M. (2013). Governance, risk management, and compliance. *Interdisciplinary Studies Journal*, 3(1), 107-110.

"Suing about say on pay". (2013). *Pensions & Investments*, 41(7), 10.

Turnbull, S. (1997). Stakeholder governance. *Corporate Governance,* 1(5), 11–23.

Williamson, O., Bercovitz, J. (1997). The modern corporation as an efficiency instrument: The comparative contracting perspective. In C. Kaysen (Ed.), *The American corporation today.* New York: Oxford University Press.

Chapter One
Governance

> The subjects covered in the governance chapter include
> Governance Types, Independence and Committees, Governance
> Practices, Antitakeover Provisions and Shareholder Rights,
> Bylaws, Shareholders' Meeting, Block Holders, Shareholder
> Activist and Proxy Advisory Service.

In the broadest sense, governance is the practice of leadership supporting decision-making that define expectations, grant power, or verify performance. The practice of corporate governance is a set of processes, customs, policies, and laws, affecting the way a corporation is directed, administered, or controlled. Shareholder rights, such as antitakeover provisions, block holders, or anything written in the Bylaws, affect how a board director can govern. Any board director needs to be familiar with these items, as they vary from corporation to corporation.

Governance Type

A board director should have a solid understanding about how governance applies to for-profit or nonprofit corporations (refer to figure 2).

➢ A for-profit corporation is a corporation intended to operate a business that will return a profit to the owners.

➢ A public corporation is a legal entity permitted to offer public corporation securities (e.g. stock, bonds) for sale to the general public. In most cases, these securities are offered through a stock exchange.

➢ A privately held corporation is a legal entity owned by one or more company founders or possibly their families or heirs or a small group of investors. Sometimes, employees also hold shares of private companies. Most small businesses are privately held. In the broadest sense, the term refers to any business that the state does not own.

➢ A nonprofit organization is an organization with a specific purpose, such as educational, charitable, or other enumerated purposes. A nonprofit may be a foundation, charity or other type of nonprofit organization.

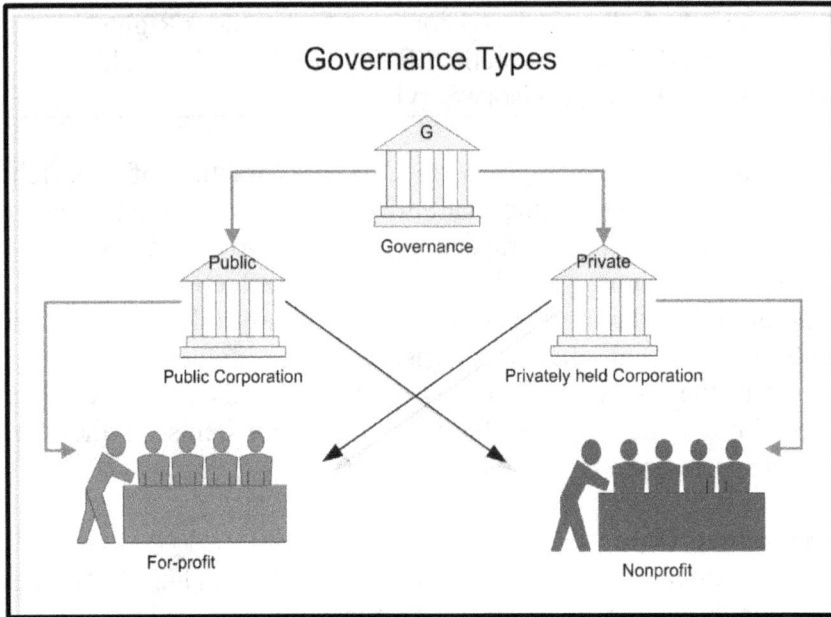

Figure 2 - Governance Types

➢ The United States Internal Revenue Code 501(c) is a special provision where twenty-eight types of nonprofit organizations are exempt from paying income tax at the federal level.[1] The IRS lists the most common 501(c) organizations, including:

501(c)	Description
(1)	❖ A corporation organized under acts of Congress
(2)	❖ Title-holding corporation for exempt organizations
(3)	❖ A charitable, nonprofit, religious, or educational organization
(4)	❖ A political education organization

(5)	❖ A labor union or agriculture organization
(6)	❖ A business league or chamber of commerce organization
(7)	❖ A recreational club organization
(8)	❖ A fraternal beneficiary society
(9)	❖ A voluntary employee beneficiary association
(10)	❖ A fraternal lodge society
(14)	❖ A credit union
(19)	❖ A U.S. veterans' post or auxiliary

Independence and Committees

➢ Researchers observed that having separate committees to nominate, compensate, audit, and govern are more effective at monitoring governance than having the board itself regulate these items.[2]

Governance Practices

➢ Governance Metrics International (GMI) is an organization dedicated to monitoring and rating corporations worldwide on several governance points. The goal of this organization is to provide an easy-to-use tool to show investors and other interested parties how effective the governance practices of a particular corporation.

➢ In 2006, researchers found that the United States ranks fourth for governance practices, but Canada, United Kingdom, and Australia placed in the top three respectively out of the forty-five countries represented in the GMI ranking.[3]

➢ Some examples of boards that fell short of shareholder expectations included General Motors, IBM, Westinghouse, Kmart, Digital Equipment Corporation, Bre X, Credit Suisse, First Boston, Credit Lyonnais, Adelphia, Paramalat, Enron, WorldCom, and Tyco.[4]

➢ In contrast, certain boards that have met shareholder expectations include Citicorp, General Electric, Warner-Lambert, TRW, KeraVision, and the Royal Bank of Canada.[5]

Antitakeover Provisions and Shareholder Rights

➢ Weak shareholder rights and the existence of anti-takeover provisions indicate weak governance. Strong and effective corporate governance is the ideal state for the board.[6]

Bylaws

➢ The bylaws contain detailed management provisions and rules for board directors, officers, and shareholders charged with corporate governance. They provide the structure and rules for governance.

➢ The bylaws include the time and place of the annual shareholder meeting; time and place of the board directors' meetings; specific modality and notices for calling special meetings; and structure for the board of directors, including the making of committees, the duties of officers and board directors, voting and quorum provisions, and many others.[7]

Shareholder Meeting

➢ A shareholder meeting is a gathering of all the shareholders of a corporation in order to elect the board of directors and hear reports on the company's business performance. A shareholder meeting is usually held annually, but a shareholder meeting can be held more frequently. This meeting is part of good governance because the board is accountable to the shareholders.

➢ United States Securities and Exchange Commission (SEC) continues to look into strengthening shareholder rights to help preserve the integrity of the board director position as well as ensure more effective corporate governance through shareholder accountability and board transparency.[8]

➢ Block holders and other influential shareholder groups can influence decisions at the shareholder meeting. Block holders have a controlling interest in a company. They have enough control over a block of voting shares so that no one stockholder or coalition of stockholders can successfully oppose a motion.

- ✓ Chairman/CEO duality tends to have fewer outside or independent directors on the board as well as lower block holder ownership.[9]
- ✓ Researchers found that block holders might be good monitors or try to influence the management for their own interest.
- ✓ Some block holders might have more incentive to monitor than others.[10]
- ✓ A board member should be aware of block holders and if the block holders' agenda is consistent with effective governance practices.

- ➤ Influential shareholder groups support majority voting or proxy advisory. Among the influential shareholder groups in the United States supporting majority voting are the proxy advisory corporation Institutional Shareholder Services (ISS), CalPERS, and the Council of Institutional Investors.

Shareholder Activist
- ➤ A shareholder activist is a person who attempts to use his or her rights as a shareholder of a publicly-traded corporation to bring about social change.
- ➤ The Board has only four options to choose from when responding to a shareholder activist including 1) seek omission of the resolution, 2) let the resolution go to a vote by all shareholders, 3) acquiesce to the social activist request for policy change or action, and 3) engage in dialogue with the shareholder activist group.[11]
- ➤ Global Proxy Watch tracks shareowner activism across borders and initiatives by companies, governments and stock exchanges to reform or block corporate governance.[12]

Proxy Advisory Service
- ➤ Proxy voting is the process by which an owner of a security provides the authority or power for a person to act on his or her behalf in voting corporate shares of stock.[13]
- ➤ Proxy advisory companies wield enormous influence in shareholder elections, as their institutional clients--primarily

mutual funds and pension plans--have significant stock holdings compared to other investors.

➢ Unfortunately, these companies are not subject to any required disclosures or oversight regarding their ability to control or influence the outcome of a vote.

➢ Some advisory services also have an inherent conflict of interest in the voting process because they also provide related consulting services, such as corporate governance ratings, corporate governance advice, and other research services, in addition to providing voting recommendations on proposals submitted in shareholder elections.

➢ Major Proxy Advisory Service Companies:

✓ RiskMetrics (ISS).[14]
✓ Egan-Jones Proxy Services.[15]
✓ Glass Lewis & Co.[16]
✓ Marco Consulting Group.[17]

ENDNOTES

1. See "Charities and Nonprofits" (2007).
2. Klein (1998); Newman and Mozes (1999); Shivdasani and Yermack (1999); Gillan Hartzell and Starks (2003).
3. Holstein (2006).
4. Morris, Brotherridge, and Urbanski (2005).
5. Morris, Brotherridge, and Urbanski (2005).
6. Gompers, Ishii, and Metrick (2003).
7. Cheeseman (2003).
8. Creech (2006).
9. Bekiris (2013).
10. Bhojraj and Sengupta (2003); Cremers and Nair (2003).
11. Rehbein, Logsdon, Van Buren (2013).
12. See http://www.proxywatch.com for more information.
13. Edelman (2013).
14. See http://www.issgovernance.com for more information.
15. See http://www.ejproxy.com for more information.
16. See http://www.glasslewis.com for more information.
17. See http://www.marcoconsulting.com for more information.

REFERENCES

Bhojraj, S., and P. Sengupta. (2003). Effect of Corporate Governance on Bond Ratings and Yields: The Role of Institutional Investors and Outside Directors. *Journal of Business,* 76, 455–475.

Charities and Nonprofits. (2007). Internal Revenue Service.

Cheeseman, H. (2003). *Contemporary Business and E-Commerce Law.* 4th ed., New Jersey: Person Education.

Creech, D. (2006). Sarbanes-Oxley and Cost Engineering. *Cost Engineering,* 48(7), 8–12.

Edelman, S. (2013). Proxy advisory firms: A guide for regulatory reform. *Emory Law Journal,* 62(5), 1369-1409.

Bekiris F., (2013) Ownership structure and board structure: are corporate governance mechanisms interrelated? *Corporate Governance*, 13(4), 352 – 364.

Gillan, L., Hartzell, J., Starks, L. (2003). *Explaining Corporate Governance: Boards, Bylaws and Charter Provisions*. Working paper.

Gompers, P., Ishii, J., Metrick, A. (2003). Corporate Governance and Equity Prices. *Quarterly Journal of Economics*, 118, 107–155.

Holstein, W. (2006). GMI rates governance by country. *Directorship* 11.

Klein, A. (1998). Company Performance and Board Committee Structure. *Journal of Law and Economics*, 41, 275–303.

Morris, J., Brotherridge, C., Urbanski, J. (2005). Bringing humility to leadership: Antecedents and consequences of leader humility. *Human Relations*, 58(10), 1323–1350.

Rehbein, K., Logsdon, J. M., & Van Buren, H.,J. (2013). Corporate responses to shareholder activists: Considering the dialogue alternative. *Journal of Business Ethics*, 112(1), 137-154.

Shivdasani, A., Yermack, D. (1999). CEO Involvement in the Selection of New Members: An Empirical Analysis. *Journal of Finance*, 54, 1829–1853.

Chapter Two
Board Characteristics

The subjects covered in the Board Characteristics chapter include Board Structure, Board of Directors, Board Size, Interlocked and Interconnected Boards, Succession Planning and Emergency Succession Planning.

A board director should understand the basic characteristics of the board on which he or she serves. The structure, size, and composition of the board all affect the board director's ability to govern.

Board Structure
➢ Researchers observed that a strong board structure will curb managerial incentives and allow the board, shareholders, and stock market to effectively monitor managers.[1]

Board of Directors
➢ The Board of Directors is a group of professionals who bring a breadth of skills, experience, and diversity to a company. Typically, the board will appoint one of its members to be the chair of the board of directors.
➢ When selecting a board of directors, the following questions should be addressed:

   ✓ What additional responsibilities will the board members have?
   ✓ Will they assist in promoting the company or identifying potential sources of capital?
   ✓ Will the board members also become shareholders?
   ✓ Are there any potential conflicts of interest with the candidates?
   ✓ What expertise should the board members have?
   ✓ Will they add diversity of experience and knowledge to the company?
   ✓ Will the board be compensated for meetings and/or paid a board director's fee?

Board Size

➢ Board size can affect governance. Smaller boards are more effective because they experience fewer communication and coordination problems. Researchers found several additional items related to board size:[2]

  ✓ From 1988 to 1999, the median board size was nine.
  ✓ The target board size for an American publicly traded company is between eight and eleven board directors.
  ✓ When the chief executive officer (CEO) is older, the board size increases.
  ✓ The CEO ownership, CEO as founder, and CEO involvement in board director selection tends to shrink the board size.
  ✓ The board size is proportional to the company size (as measured by total assets).

➢ Researchers observed that, contrary to popular belief, effective governance and good financial performance is not necessarily linked to the number of external board directors.[3]

Interlocked and Interconnected Boards

An interesting situation among board membership is when boards become interlocked or interconnected (refer to figure 3).

➢ When two CEOs from different companies sit on each other's boards, then the situation is said that the two boards are interlocked.

  ✓ The fear with interlocked boards is that the CEOs can mutually support each other's agenda, including possibly their compensation package and more favorable consideration. They could also possibly influence the selection of new board directors and hinder the ability to facilitate social cohesion among other board directors.

➢ When two or more board directors sit on the same multiple boards, then those boards are said to be "interconnected."
➢ Interconnected boards may point to groups of board directors having a different focus besides the interests of shareholders.

> Researchers suggest that board of directors filled with board director appointees who are sympathetic to the CEO are likely to overcompensate and under monitor the chief executive.[4]
> The same researchers suggest that mutually interlocking board directorships that are prevalent among corporations are responsible for the production of sympathetic board directors.

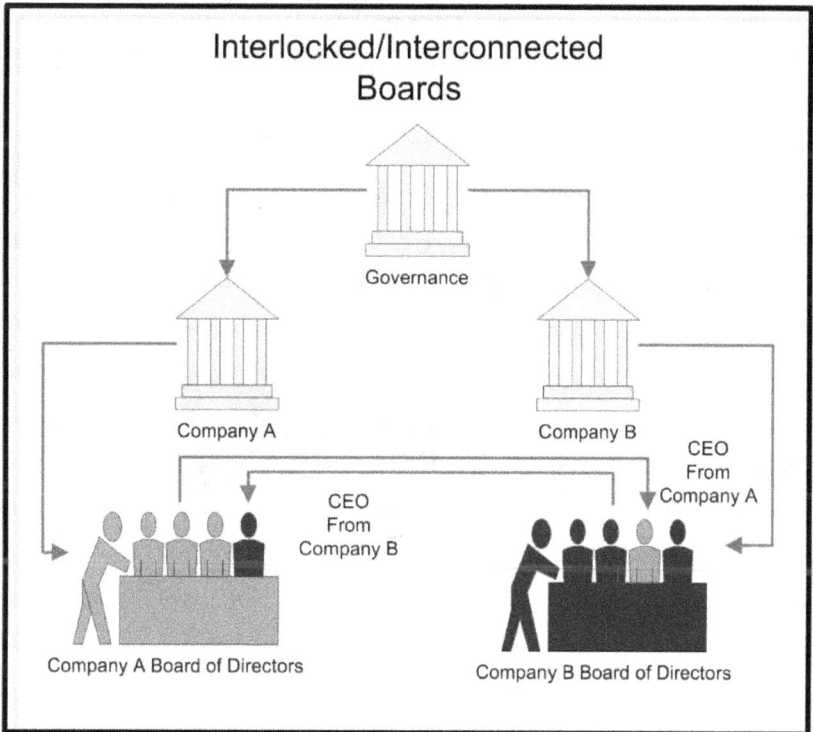

Figure 3-Interlocked/Interconnected Boards

Succession Planning

➤ Succession planning is planning who will fill board positions that become vacant, for example, the CEO, senior executive team, and the board itself.

➤ Success planning should be the responsibility of the lead board director. [5]

➤ Succession planning also involves reviewing board composition. Being aware that knowing who will fill key positions (should they become vacant) keeps the organization moving toward organizational goals.

➤ CEO succession planning deserves more time and attention by the board of directors.[6]

➤ More progressive boards are shifting from the short-term, tactical recruiting of board directors to a longer-term strategic approach to building boards in response to the direction and needs of the business.

Emergency Succession Planning

➤ Make sure to have already identified a single individual who would be able to assume the CEO role just in case of an emergency situation.

➤ At least two internal individuals should be identified who are qualified to serve as CEO in an emergency situation.[7]

ENDNOTES

1. Ertugrual and Hedge (2005).
2. Yermack (1996).
3. Yermack (1996).
4. Fich and White (2004).
5. See "Planning for CEO succession" (2013).
6. Field (2013).
7. See "Planning for CEO succession" (2013).

REFERENCES

Ertugrul, M., Hedge, S. (2005). *Corporate Governance and Company Performance*. Financial Management Association.

Fich, E., White, L. (2004). *Ties that Bind*. Stern Business School, New York University.

Field, G. (2013, Apr 27). Planning for succession? *The Nation*.

Planning for CEO succession. (2013). *The Corporate Governance Advisor*, 21(5), 1-10.

Yermack, D. (1996). Higher Market Valuation of Companies with a Small Board of Directors. *Journal of Financial Economic* 40: 185–211.

Chapter Three
Board Director Characteristics

> The subjects covered in the Board Director Characteristics chapter include Activities Prior to Joining a Board, Types of Board Directors, Term of Board Directors, Recruitment of Board Directors, Notable Board Directors Listings, Board Director Qualifications, Board Director Expertise, Board Director Leadership Skills, Transformational Leadership and Innovation: A Personal Leadership Plan, Board Director Trustworthiness, Personal Knowledge Management, Board Director Professionalism, Ethics Applied: Insider Trading, and Board Directors and Officers Liability Insurance.

A person awarded a position on a company's board should feel both a sense of honor and obligation to the board director position.

Board directors monitor a company's financial performance and the success of its products, services, and strategy. They are expected to follow developments that affect the business and set aside any potential conflict between their personal or individual business interests to support the well-being of the business that they serve. Ideally, board directors should have backgrounds and contacts that differ from, but complement, the background of the officers of the company and other board directors. The most effective board is a group of professionals who bring a breadth of skills, experience, and diversity to a company.

Key components to a successful board are board directors with leadership skills, trustworthiness, and good business ethics.

Activities Prior to Joining a Board
> ➤ Consider gathering and reviewing the following items before taking on the responsibility of joining a board:

  - ✓ A description of the members' responsibilities.
  - ✓ A brief biography of the CEO.
  - ✓ A list of the current board members, titles, and associated board member affiliations.

- ✓ A board organizational chart.
- ✓ The company's most recent audited financial statements.
- ✓ The long-range road map and financial plan.
- ✓ A company's annual report.
- ✓ A company's or organization's newsletter, brochure, or any available publications.

➢ Evaluate the board directors' tenure, that is, the amount of time a person holds a governance position at a company.

- ✓ A board director's tenure can be viewed as an important indicator of effective corporate governance.
- ✓ Researchers observed that senior board directors are more likely to make decisions favoring management.[1]

Types of Board Directors

➢ A board director is a person chosen to govern the affairs of a corporation or other large institution.

- ✓ A board director may be an inside director, that is, a director who is also an officer, or an outside, or independent, director (refer to figure 4).

Types of Directors

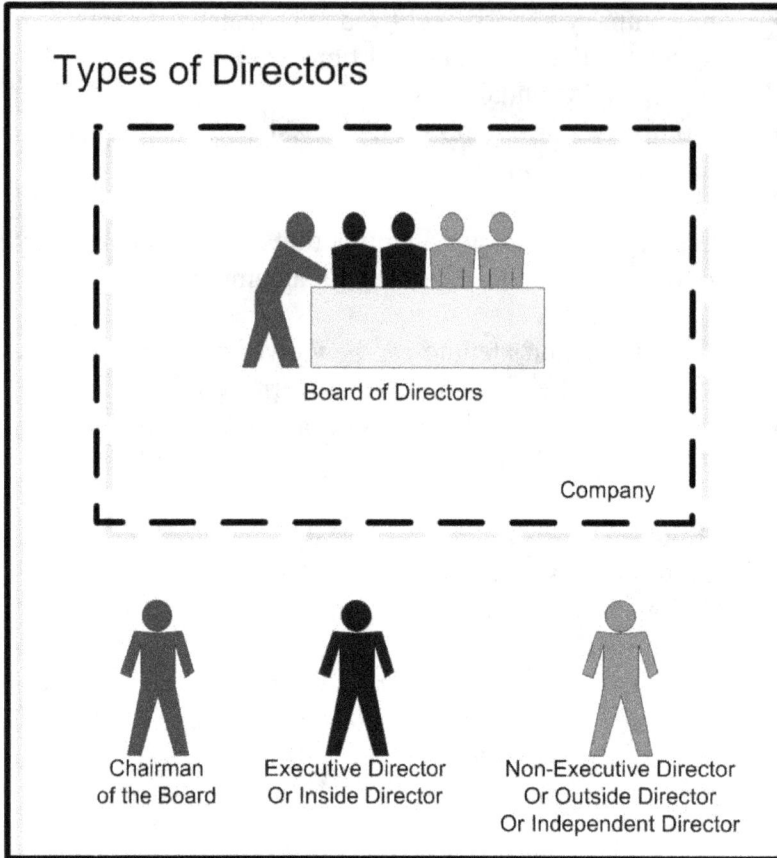

Figure 4-Board of Directors

> ➤ An executive director is a person dedicated full-time to his or her role in relation to the management of the company.
> ➤ A non-executive director, or independent director, is considered to be an outsider to the company.
> ➤ The independent director position is typically held by a person who is not part of the management of a company.

> ✓ He or she is brought in for his or her expertise.
> ✓ He or she also lends a more impartial view in relation to strategic decision.
> ✓ Over the last decade, many private companies are asking "Independent Board Directors" to join the board of directors, especially for "Venture Capital" backed companies.

- ✓ A "best practice" is to have a minimum of three outside (or independent) board directors on the board of directors.
- ✓ A board with a majority of independent board directors is more effective in monitoring the management than a board with a minority of independent board directors.[2]
- ✓ In the situation when a company prepares for an Initial Public Offering (IPO) or sale, a "best practice" is to have an "Independent Board Director" chair each of the following committees including audit, compensation, human resources, governance and technology (especially for those companies in the technology industry).

- ➤ The chairperson of the board, the presiding board director over the other board directors on the board, leads the board of directors.
- ➤ The chairman/CEO duality is when a single person is both chairman of the board and CEO (refer to figure 5).

  - ✓ Costs of separating these roles between chairman and CEO by assigning these roles to different people outweigh the benefits.[3]
  - ✓ In contrast, chairman/CEO duality has the strongest effect on governance policies when a powerful CEO holds both positions.[4]
  - ✓ Chairman/CEO duality tends to have fewer outside or independent directors on the board as well as lower block holder ownership.[5]

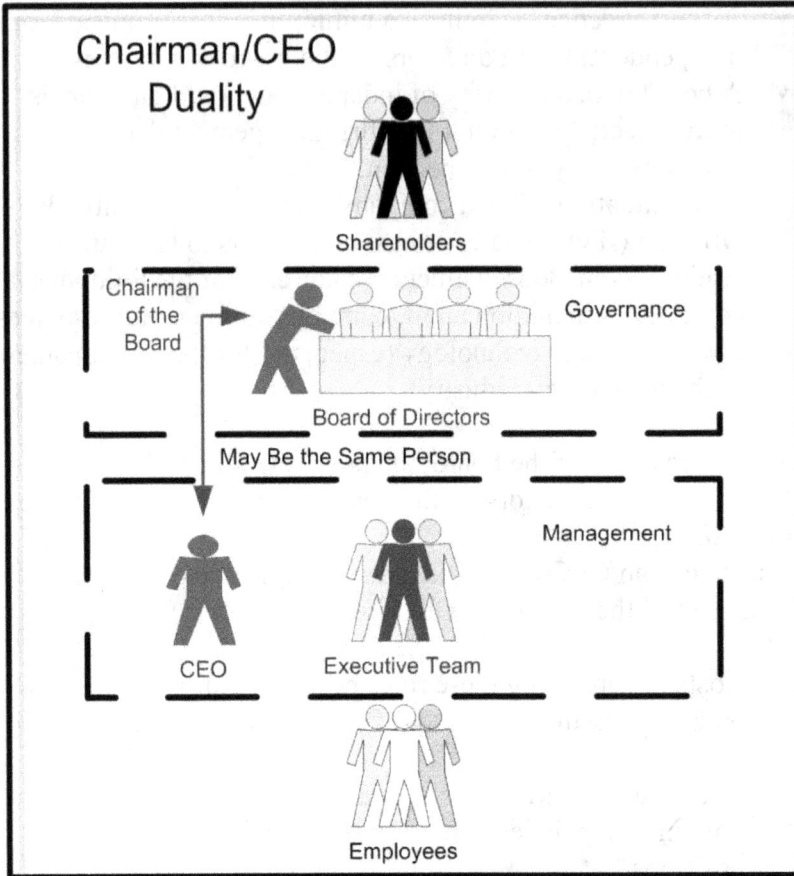

Figure 5-Chairman and CEO Duality

A Board Directors' Term Limit
➤ The board directors' term limit is typically for one year between annual shareholder meetings, unless the articles of incorporation allow for a staggered.[6]

Board Director Recruitment
➤ Boards are shifting to more independent board directors. Board director recruitment is on the rise because the board directors' requirements are becoming more complex.
➤ Active Chief Executive Officers are taking on fewer directorships.

- ➢ Boards increasingly see recruiting as an opportunity to add someone with a defined set of skills and experience that will improve a board's ability to support the strategy.
- ➢ Finding board directors with technology or marketing expertise as well as international background is the trend.

  - ✓ Additionally, the numbers of women and minority board directors still fall short of the levels desired by boards within the United States.

C-Level Management

- ➢ Describes high-ranking executive titles within an organization.
- ➢ C in this context refers to Chief such as CEO (Chief Executive Officer), CIO (Chief Information Officer, CISO (Chief Information Security Officer), COO (Chief Operating Officer), CFO (Chief Finance Officer).
- ➢ An officer of the company and part of the executive team.

Notable Board Director Listings

- ➢ Given the increased responsibility and Sarbanes-Oxley (SOX) compliance, selecting the right board director is becoming harder to do since there is a shortage qualified board directors.
- ➢ A number of board director sources are available to find a particular board director.

  - ✓ The notable board director listing services include Hoovers.[7]

Board Director Qualifications

- ➢ A set of board director qualifications establish the standard from which a board director candidate must be judged in order to hold a governance position.
- ➢ Board director qualifications vary among companies. However, a general set of qualifications demonstrating include

  - ✓ Notable or significant achievements in business, education, or public service.
  - ✓ Possessing the requisite intelligence, education, and experience to make a significant contribution to the board.

- ✓ Bringing a range of skills as well as diverse perspectives and backgrounds.
- ✓ Possessing the highest ethical standards, a strong sense of professionalism, and intense dedication to serving the interests of the stockholders.

➤ The following attributes or qualifications will be considered by the governance in evaluating a person's candidacy for membership on the board:

- ✓ A past or current leadership role in a major public company or recognized privately held entity.
- ✓ A past or current leadership role at a prominent educational institution or senior faculty position in an area of study important or relevant to the company.
- ✓ A past elected or appointed senior government position or current senior managerial or advisory position with a highly visible nonprofit organization.

➤ Skilled and diverse background must possess the aptitude or experience and should include, at a minimum, the following:

- ✓ A full understanding of the legal responsibilities of a board director and the governance processes of a public company.
- ✓ The personal qualities to be able to make a substantially active contribution to board deliberations.
- ✓ Self-assuredness, interpersonal and communication skills, as well as courage and inquisitiveness.

➤ When serving on an audit committee consideration should be given to financial management, reporting, and control expertise or other experience that would qualify the candidate as a "financial expert" under established standards and international experience.

➤ Essential characteristics for each board member include

- ✓ Highest standards of moral and ethical character.
- ✓ Highest personal integrity.
- ✓ Highest independence.
- ✓ Highest objectivity.
- ✓ Intense dedication to serve as a representative of the stockholders.
- ✓ A personal commitment to the company's principles and values.
- ✓ Impeccable corporate governance credentials.

Board Director's Expertise

➤ A board collectively possesses the transformational influence that establishes the value-based climate through which ethical values, ethical conduct, legal compliance, and social responsibility significantly influences employees' attitudes and behaviors as well as shareholder perception.[8]

➤ Domain knowledge is a board director's accumulation of expertise in particular subject areas based on his or her experience, education, and skills.

➤ A board director's expertise consists of both life experience and of domain knowledge and requires the board director to understand decision-making from various perspectives (in addition to his or her domain knowledge).

➤ A leader's ability to simplify a complex problem is an excellent way to address to speed of change as well as a greater ability to cope with change.[9]

- ✓ Common board director knowledge domains include accounting, advertising, competitor intelligence, core product technology, corporate governance, distribution/logistics, engineering, finance, general management, governmental relations, international business, human resources, information technology, labor relations, legal compliance, marketing research, product development, production, public relations, research and development, sales, shareholder relations, and turnaround.

Board Director's Leadership Skills
➢ Leadership is the ability to influence, motivate, and enable others to contribute toward the effectiveness of the organization of which they are members.
➢ A leader's knowledge of his or her organization's needs results in better decision-making associated with operational knowledge of the human resource drivers on performance, technology investments, process improvements, and overall business intelligence (BI).
➢ A distinguishing factor between leadership and management is that effective leadership precedes effective management.[10]
➢ A board director, as a leader, must involve the right people in the decision, at the right time, and in the right way; use a process that keeps people engaged and on track; recognize the power of shared decision making; and ask a series of key questions to avoid ineffective decision making.[11]
➢ Leadership and management are both stressful during times of economic downturns, but this environment presents an opportunity for optimizing operations.[12]
➢ Having a deep operational knowledge of an organization enables the manager to leverage existing resources thereby realizing previously untapped potential operational value.[13]

Leadership Styles
➢ A director should become familiar with different leadership styles by comparing and contrasting the Pre-Classical, Classical, Modernism, and Post-Modernism era of leadership models against his or her leadership styles.

Pre-Classical Leadership
➢ The Pre-Classical era (between 1910 to World War II) defines leadership as the universal formula of the traits period.[14]
➢ During this time, leadership depended on the study of people who were already great leaders, typically from the aristocracy, and perpetuating the notion that leadership had something to do with good breeding or their traits.

   ✓ In other words, the universal approach assumes that there is "one best way" to lead in all situations.

➢ Leaders possess certain traits including

✓ Intelligence.
✓ Task relevant knowledge.
✓ Dominance.
✓ Self-confidence.
✓ Energy.
✓ Tolerance for stress.
✓ Integrity and honesty.
✓ Emotional maturity.

Classical Leadership

➢ The Classical era defines two periods of importance— behavior and contingency.[15]
➢ Between the start of World War II to late 1960's defined leadership as the behavior period
➢ Between the late 1960's to mid-1980's defined leadership as the contingency period
➢ In 1948, Ralph Stogi lll concluded that traits alone do not identify leadership.[16]
➢ The behavioral approach emphasized the observable behavior that makes a leader effective
➢ The Managerial Grid represents two dimensions used in this model—concern for production and concern for people—to examine leadership behavior and characteristics.
➢ The Managerial Grid has its advantages and disadvantages. The Managerial Grid focuses on observable actions of the leader in order to determine if the leader's main concern is for production or for people.

✓ This provides a more reliable method for studying leadership than the trait approach
✓ The Managerial Grid, however, adopted the universal approach. The Managerial Grid aims at identifying the most effective leadership style for all situations, not supported by evidence in real organizations. [17]

➢ A prominent theory is the Fiedler's contingency theory.

- ➢ Fred Fiedler believes that leadership effectiveness depends on both the leader's personality and the situation.
- ➢ Certain leaders are effective in one situation but not in others.
- ➢ The Least Preferred Coworker (LPC) scale used to measure a leader's motivation.

  - ✓ Task motivation compared to relationship motivation.

- ➢ More importantly, these are the trait versions of the concern of production compared to concern of people categories in the Managerial Grid
- ➢ Another contingency theory is the Path-Goal theory
- ➢ Path-Goal theory is different from Fiedler's Contingent Theory in that Path-Goal theory focuses on the situation and leader behavior rather than leader personality traits
- ➢ Path-Goal leadership styles include directive, supportive, participative and achievement-oriented
- ➢ Yet another contingency theory is the Hersey-Blanchard situational leadership model where effective leaders vary style with follower readiness
- ➢ Hersey-Blanchard situational leadership model proposes that the optimal style of supervision in terms of a combination of relationship-oriented behavior and task-oriented behavior changes as the level of follower maturity increases.

- ➢ The leader's style includes telling, selling, participating and delegating.[18]
- ➢ Leadership substitutes are contingencies that limit a leader's influence or make a particular leadership style unnecessary

  - ✓ For example, self-leadership replaces achievement-oriented leadership.

Modernism Leadership
- ➢ The Modernism era between the mid 1980's and late 1990's defines leadership as the team leadership period.[19]
- ➢ The emphasis is on the process of team leadership where team leadership places more ownership and responsibility on all of the team members instead of the leader alone.

- From coaching and training to developing a learning environment to managing boundaries, team leadership results in effective leadership when team members are empowered.[20]
- A significant contribution during the period was Bass's introduction of both transactional and transformational leadership that included seven leadership factors including[20]

  - ✓ charisma,
  - ✓ inspirational,
  - ✓ intellectual stimulation,
  - ✓ individualized consideration,
  - ✓ contingent reward,
  - ✓ management-by-exception,
  - ✓ Laisse faire leadership.

- However, Burns made a refinement between two types of leadership he termed transactional and transformational (refer to table 1).

Transactional Leader	Transformational Leader
❖ Managing – relationship between job performance to reward	❖ Leading – changing the organization to fit the environment
❖ Ensure employee have necessary resources	❖ A change agent
❖ Apply contingency style of leadership	

Table 1-Transactional Leader versus Transformational Leader

- Transformational leadership raises the level of human conduct of both leader and follower.
- Transformational leaders throw themselves into a dynamic relationship with followers who will feel elevated by the relationship and become more active themselves, thereby creating new cadres of leaders.[22]

Post-Modernism Leadership

- The Post-Modernism era between the late 1990's and the present defines leadership as facilitating leadership.[23]

➢ By facilitating leadership, the emphasis is on the leader providing a shared vision, ensuring alignment the relationship, and an ability to unlock the personal qualities of others.

➢ Charismatic leadership is a leader that has the ability that includes

  ✓ vision and articulation,
  ✓ personal risk,
  ✓ environmental sensitivity,
  ✓ sensitive to follower needs,
  ✓ unconventional behavior,
  ✓ Self-confidence.
  ✓ strong convictions about the vision

➢ Followers enjoy being with the charismatic leader because they feel inspired, correct and important.
➢ Visionary leadership is the ability of a leader:

  ✓ to create and articulate a realistic, credible attractive vision of the future for an organization,
  ✓ to explain the vision to others,
  ✓ to express the vision not just verbally but through the leader's behavior and can extend the vision in different leadership contexts.

➢ Visionary leadership and charismatic leadership are different if only by personality traits.
➢ "Visionary leaders share certain characteristics that are different from the personality traits on which early leadership research was focused." [24]
➢ Effective leaders mentor leadership.
➢ The leader exhibits:

  ✓ a personal interest in the leadership behaviors of others,
  ✓ teaching leadership as the leader practices leading,
  ✓ encouraging to practice leadership from the heart,
  ✓ fostering collaboration through the relinquishing of power.

> For example, the spirit of effective leadership in the Post-Modernism era with the following:[25]

  ✓ adaptive demands of our time require leaders who take responsibility without waiting for reevaluation or request. One can lead with no more than a question in hand.

Leadership Effectiveness
> What is leadership?

  ✓ Leadership is the ability to influence, motivate, and enable others to contribute toward the effectiveness of the organizations of which they are members.
  ✓ Leaders do not necessary need to be in a formal leadership position to exert leadership behavior.
  ✓ An effective leader is someone who motivates a person or a group to accomplish more than they would have otherwise accomplished without that leader's involvement.
  ✓ To assess the leadership styles in terms of effectiveness for its originating timeframe, we need to review the evolution path leadership has taken over the years.
  ✓ For example, in retrospect, a flaw existed with thinking that traits consistently were associated with great leadership since ignoring the situational and environmental factors play a role in a leader's level of effectiveness.[26]

> By moving beyond the notion that leadership was an inborn trait, our attention can be focused on the possibility that an effective leadership method can be taught to anyone.

  ✓ Pushing this notion even further enabled answering a critical question that lead to the idea that not only the interaction between the leader's traits, the leader's behaviors were important to understanding leadership, but also the situation in which the leader exists was important as well.
  ✓ Hence, the contingency theory was born and a more realistic view of leadership emerged that allowed for the complexity

and situational components of the overall effectiveness of leadership to be addressed.

➢ So how could leadership become more effective?

✓ For leaders to be effective, issues related to an organization's culture would need to be clearly exposed.
✓ This required that some additional skills were required for leaders in order to manage the organizational culture.
✓ Leaders were not only involved in managing the culture through strategic direction, but also defining the organizational vision and values.

➢ So what is motivating these leaders?

✓ This is when motivation theories come in to being by asking the question how could leaders influence others' behavior?

Leadership Comparison
➢ A comparison of the different leadership styles helps to elicit insight about each of the styles.

➢ Some of the questions that are answered with this comparison consist of

✓ How different leadership styles' origins have shaped them.
✓ Points where leadership styles converge or diverge.
✓ Similarities or differences in the application of these leadership styles.
✓ A rating for each of the leadership style's ability to address contemporary leadership environments.
✓ Over time different leadership styles' appeared and were shaped by various influential factors as leadership was evolving.
✓ How different leadership styles' origins have shaped them (refer to table 2).

Era	Period	Leadership Style Characteristic	Shaped by influential factors
Pre Classical	1910 to World War II	Universal formula of traits	People who were already great leaders, control and centralization of power
Classical	World War II to mid-1980's	Behavior and Contingency	People who were already great leaders
Modernism	mid 1980's and late 1990's	Team Leadership	Limited sharing of leadership with others
Post Modernism	late 1990's and the present	Facilitating Leadership	Limited sharing of leadership with others

Table 2-Leadership Styles

➤ Over time, there were points where leadership styles converge or diverge.
➤ Converge is when leadership styles within the period start to overlap (refer to table 3).

Era	Period	Leadership Style	Same	Different
Pre Classical	1910 to World War II	Universal formula of traits	X	
Classical	World War II to mid-1980's	Managerial Grid, Fiedler's Contingency, Path-Goal, Situational	X	
Modernism	mid 1980's and late 1990's	Transactional, transformational		X
Post Modernism	late 1990's and the present	Charismatic, visionary	X	

Table 3-Leadership Styles Convergence and Divergence

➤ Over time, there were similarities or differences in the application of these leadership styles (refer to table 4).

Era	Period	Leader Style	Same	Different
Pre Classical	1910 to World War II	universal formula of traits	Leadership can be taught	Traits are subjective
Classical	World War II to mid-1980's	Managerial Grid, Fiedler's Contingency, Path-Goal, Situational	Situational and environmental factors	Managerial Grid focus on most effective leadership style for all situations where Fiedler's Contingency and Path-Goal are similar
Modernism	mid 1980's and late 1990's	Transactional, transformational	Organizational culture	Focus has almost exclusively been on the transformational, not transactional
Post Modernism	late 1990's and the present	Charismatic, visionary	Influence others' behavior	personality traits differ; charisma is hard to define

Table 4-Leadership Differences

➤ A rating was derived for each of the style's ability to address contemporary leadership environments on a scale between (refer to table 5).

✓ 1 and 10.
✓ 1 is poor capability to address contemporary leadership environments.
✓ 10 is high capability to address contemporary leadership environments.

Era	Period	Leadership Style	Ability to address contemporary leadership environments
Pre Classical	1910 to World War II	universal formula of the traits	1
Classical	World War II to mid-1980's	Managerial Grid, Fiedler's Contingency, Path-Goal, Situational leadership	5
Modernism	mid 1980's and late 1990's	Transactional, transformatio nal	6
Post Modernism	late 1990's and the present	Charismatic, visionary	8

Table 6-Capability Ranking to Address Contemporary Leadership Environments

Transformational Leadership and Innovation: A Personal Leadership Plan

➢ The Transformational Leadership Model.
➢ A transformational leader is someone who can see the big picture.
➢ One such person is Bill Gates.

✓ His role was of Chief Architect at Microsoft placing a huge burden on his shoulders.
✓ Some might say that Bill Gates has not only shaped the computer industry through his leadership at Microsoft but also he has provided countless opportunities to other individuals who have themselves started companies of their own to bring innovation to market.
✓ Interestingly, today companies not thought as innovative actually had someone who could see the big picture leading the company.
✓ In all, only three of the visionary companies began life with the benefit of a specific, innovative, and highly successful initial product or service—a "great idea": Johnson and Johnson, General Electric, and Ford.[27]
✓ A leader's ability to maintain focus on the big picture while, in some sense, the entire world tries to prove the leader wrong is what transformational leadership is all about.
✓ In this case, Bill Gates is a transformational leader who has a very broad reach.
✓ A strong case exists for adopting a transformational strategy as a way to bring about "significant and needed change in individuals, teams, and the organization as a whole."[28]
✓ Champions exhibited higher risk taking and innovativeness, initiated more influence attempts, and used a greater variety of influence tactics than a non-champion.
✓ Practicing transformational leadership, an effective leader can become an outstanding leader but should consider taking some risk in order to cultivate innovation.

➢ Features of Outstanding Leaders
   ✓ An effective leader mentors leadership.
   ✓ The leader exhibits a personal interest in the leadership behaviors of others, teaching leadership as the leader practices, encouraging practicing leadership from the heart, and fostering collaboration through the relinquishing of power. [29]
   ✓ In order to understand what it takes to be an outstanding leader a brief recap of the essences of leadership.

➢ Transformational Leadership is Different from Transactional leadership
   ✓ Transactional leadership is characterized by the mutual dependence between leader and follower.
   ✓ For example, horse trading one thing for another thing comes to mind when thinking about transactional leadership. [30]
   ✓ In contrast, transformational leadership is about unifying followers and changing the followers' goals and possibly their beliefs.
   ✓ For example, transformational leadership (symbolic leadership) is very powerful, in that, transformation leadership's purpose can be put to both good and bad use.
   ✓ A demonstration of good use was by Franklin D. Roosevelt when he reassured a nation in deep economic depression.

➢ Four Characteristics of Transformational Leadership
➢ Four characteristics of transformational leadership but also the necessary characteristics of an outstanding leader
➢ Transformational leadership requires four recognizable and repeatable leadership strategies including[31]

   ✓ Idealized influence.
   ✓ Inspirational motivation.
   ✓ Intellectual stimulation.
   ✓ Individualized consideration.

- ➢ The Personal Leadership Plan
  - ✓ A leader's leadership style changes over time.
  - ✓ A leader's leadership style can take on multiple styles over time.
  - ✓ In order to develop a leadership plan a leader must first understand leadership, his or her leadership style and then his or her leadership's role in innovation.
  - ✓ Best way to go about this is for a leader to be reflective and for the leader to put in writing a personal leadership plan – next 6 months, 12 months and 3 years and beyond.
  - ✓ Most important – a leader should periodically look at the personal leadership plan for tracking purpose and take time out to make any course corrections or to change behavior.

Board Director Trustworthiness and Leadership Confidence
- ➢ A board director needs to be both trustworthy and embody a leadership confidence in others with his or her leadership skills. For example, an ethical based decision for a board director is whether to endorse or hinder the pursuit by a company's management team with off balance sheet (OBS) financing. OBS is an asset or debt or financing activity not on the company's balance sheet that allows for possible misrepresentation of the company's financial structure to creditors, shareholders, and the public. Other important duties required by the governance position include (refer to table 7).

Duty of Obedience	❖ A board director must obey the law and regulations giving them the authority to manage a corporation.
Duty of Care	❖ A board director must use prudent judgment and act with ordinary good faith in self-judgment.
Duty of Loyalty	❖ A board director must put his or her personal interests after the corporate interest.

Table 7-Duties Required

Personal Knowledge Management (PKM):

➤ A collection of processes that an individual needs to carry out in order to gather, classify, store, search, and retrieve knowledge in his/her daily activities.

➤ How board directors apply knowledge processes to support their day-to-day work activities

➤ Integrates personal information management (PIM), focused on individual skills, with knowledge management (KM).

Board Director Professionalism

➤ A board director must incorporate business ethics as part of his or her decision making because business ethics concentrate on moral standards that apply to business policies, institutions, and behavior.[32]

➤ Ethics is the study of morality or moral standards.[33]

➤ Ethics are used daily to motivate a person to do the right thing.[34]

➤ Morality is the study of standards for either an individual or a group.[35]

➤ Virtue ethics is when a person is typically motivated to do the right thing for all stakeholders and takes action. Virtue ethics drives desirable character traits in a person.[36] Virtue ethics supports the greatest good for the overall collective.[37]

   ✓ For example, various ethical challenges present themselves daily, surfacing as a conflict between self and others. A board director will come across challenges between personal and professional responsibility. A board director must acknowledge that virtue ethics supports corporate governance with an eye on creating the greatest good for the stakeholder collective. Researchers have found that virtue ethics drives desirable character traits in a person.[38]

➤ While situational ethics take into account both action and context (or situation for the action), virtue ethics focus solely on the action, regardless of context.

Ethics Applied: Insider Trading

➢ Insider trading is the trading of securities by corporate insiders, such as a board director, corporate officer, key employee, or holder of more than 10 percent of the company's shares.[39]

➢ Restrictions for insider trading occur during the blackout period, that is, any period where the beneficiary of the defined contribution plans are temporarily suspended to purchase, sell, acquire, or transfer securities.

✓ The beneficiary is a board director or executive officer who is restricted from trading stock that the individual acquired during his or her service a member of the company's board of directors or employed as an executive officer during any blackout period.

Board Directors' and Officers' Liability Insurance

➢ Both board directors and officers potentially incur risk by taking a position on a company's board as well as taking on the accountability associated with the outcome of his or her governance decision making.

✓ Board directors' and officers' liability insurance (D and O) offers individual board directors and officers the protection they need from personal liability and financial loss arising from wrongful acts committed or allegedly committed in their capacity as corporate (parent organization and subsidiaries) officers or board directors.

✓ Most D and O policies also cover the liability of the corporate entity itself if the liability arises out of a claim involving the purchase or sale of the company's securities.

✓ Researchers found that the optimal situation is for directors to be fully insured against the liability, especially, in the situation where there might be a risk for endorsing a CEO's suboptimal decisions. When D and O insurance is not paid by the business, a potential board director candidate may elect not to accept a position on the board of directors.[40]

ENDNOTES

1. Vafeas (2003).
2. Hermalin and Weisbach (2003); Klein (1998).
3. Coles and Jarrell (1997).
4. Arena and Braga-Alves (2013).
5. Bekiris (2013).
6. Cheeseman (2003).
7. See http://www.hoovers.com for more information.
8. Arjoon (2006).
9. Wong, (2003).
10. Shriberg, Shriberg, and Lloyd (2002).
11. Schwarber (2005).
12. Hay and Hodgkinson (2006).
13. Andreou et al. (2007).
14. Chemers (1984), p. 83.
15. Chemers (1984), p. 83.
16. Wren (1995), p.84.
17. Wren (1995), p.88.
18. Norris and Vecchio (1992), p. 331.
19. Chemers (1984), p. 83.
20. Horner (1997), p.285.
21. Avolio, Bass and Jung (1999), p. 442.
22. Krishnan (2001), p. 126.
23. Chemers (1984), p. 83.
24. Sashkin (1995), p. 403.
25. Heifetz and Laurie (2003), p. 557.
26. Horner (1997), p. 270.
27. Collins and Porras (1996),
28. Guns (1995), p. 340.
29. Appelbaum, Hebert and Leroux (1999), p.248.
30. Bolman and Deal (2003).
31. Bass and Avolio (1994).
32. Velasquez (1998).
33. Velasquez (1998).
34. McAdams, Freeman, and Pincus (1995).
35. Velasquez (1998).
36. McAdams, Freeman, and Pincus (1995).
37. Caldwell and Ranjan (2005).
38. McAdams, Freeman, and Pincus (1995).

39. Harris (2003).
40. MacMinn, Ren, and Han (2012).

REFERENCES

Arena, M., Braga-Alves, M. (2013). The discretionary effect of CEOs and board chairs on corporate governance structures, *Journal of Empirical Finance*, 21, 121-131.

Avolio, B. J., Bass, B. M., Jung, D. I. (1999, December). Re-examining the components of transformational and transactional leadership using the multifactor leadership questionnaire. *Journal of Occupational and Organizational Psychology*, 72, 441-462.

Andreou, A., Green, A., Stankosky, M. (2007). A framework of intangible valuation areas and antecedents, *Journal of Intellectual Capital*, 8(1), 52-75.

Appelbaum, S., Hebert, D., Leroux, S. (1999) Empowerment: power, culture and leadership – a strategy or fad for the millennium, *Journal of Workplace Learning: Employee Counseling Today*, 11(7), 248.

Arjoon, S. (2006). Striking a balance between rules and principles-based approaches for effective governance: A risks-based approach. *Journal of Business Ethics,* 68(1), 53.

Bass, B.M. and Avolio, B.J. (1994). Improving organizational effectiveness through transformational leadership. *Thousand Oaks, CA: Sage.*

Bekiris, F. (2013) Ownership structure and board structure: are corporate governance mechanisms interrelated? *Corporate Governance*, 13(4), 352 – 364.

Bolman, L., Deal, E. (2003). *Reframing organizations: Artistry, choice, and leadership.*

Brickley, J. A., Coles, J. L., & Jarrell, G. (1997). Leadership structure: Separating the CEO and chairman of the board. *Journal of corporate Finance*, *3*(3), 189-220.

Caldwell, C., Ranjan, K. (2005). Organizational governance and ethical systems: A covenantal approach to building trust. *Journal of Business Ethics*, *2*(58), 249–259.

Cheeseman, H. (2003). *Contemporary Business and E-Commerce Law*. 4th ed., New Jersey: Person Education.

Chemers, M. (1984). The Social, Organizational, and Cultural Context of Effective Leadership, *Leadership: Multidisciplinary Perspectives, 93-108.*

Collins, J. C., & Porras, J. I. (1996). Building your company's vision. *Harvard business review*, *74*(5), 65.

Guns, B. (1995). The faster learning organization (FLO). In S. Chawla & J. Rensch (Eds.), *Learning organizations: Developing cultures for tomorrow's workplace* (pp. 337-349). Portland OR: Productivity Press.

Harris, L. (2003). *Trading and Exchanges*. Oxford Press: Oxford.

Hay, A., Hodgkinson, M. (2006). Rethinking leadership: A way forward for teaching leadership? *Leadership and Organization Development Journal*, *27*(2), 144–158.

Heifetz, R. A., & Laurie, D. L. (2003). The work of leadership. *Leadership*, 35.

Hermalin, B., Weisbach, M. (2003). *Boards of Directors as an Endogenously Determined Institution: A Survey of Economic Literature*. Federal Reserve Bank of New York Economic Policy Review.

Horner, M. (1997) Leadership theory: past, present and future, *Team Performance Management*, *3*(4), 285.

Krishnan, V. R. (2001). Value systems of transformational leaders. *Leadership & Organization Development Journal*, 22(3), 126.

MacMinn, R., Ren, Y., Han, L. (2012). Directors, directors and officers insurance, and corporate governance. *Journal of Insurance Issues, 35*(2), 159-179.

McAdams, T., Freeman, J., Pincus, L. (1995). *Law, Business and Society*. 4th ed. Chicago: McGraw-Hill/Irwin.

Norris, W. R.,Vecchio, R. P. (1992, September). Situational leadership theory: A replication. *Group & Organization Management*, 17(3), 331.

Sashkin, M., (1989). Visionary leadership the perspective from education, *In Contemporary Issues in Leadership*, 2, 403.

Schwarber, P. (2005). Leaders and the decision-making process. *Management Decision,* 43(7/8), 1086–1092.

Shriberg, A., Shriberg, D. L., Kumari, R. (2005). *Practicing leadership, principles and application* (3rd ed.). New York: Wiley.

Vafeas, N. (2003). Length of Board Tenure and Outside Director Independence. *Journal of Business Finance and Accounting,* 30, 1043–1064.

Velasquez, M. (1998). *Business Ethics Concepts and Cases*. 4th ed. Upper Saddle River, N.J.: Prentice-Hall.

Wong, E. (2003). Leadership style for school-based management in Hong Kong, *The International Journal of Education Management,* 17(6), 243–247.

Wren, J. T. (1995). *The leader's companion insights on leadership through the ages*, New York: The Free Press.

Chapter Four
Celebrity Board Director

> The subjects covered in the Celebrity Board Director chapter include Leadership, Celebrity Board Director, Notable Celebrity Board Directors, Celebrity Board Director or Not, Celebrity Credibility, Celebrity Goodwill, Celebrity Rights, Celebrity Standard of Value, Celebrity Image, Celebrity Influence, and Celebrity Liability, Other Celebrity Board Director Characteristics, and Monetizing Celebrity.

A celebrity is defined as a famous person or a person who is widely known both in society and in the business community who commands a degree of public and media attention. A celebrity possesses one or more traits of the following traits: credibility, goodwill, rights, image, influence, liabilities, and standard of value.[1] Appointment of a celebrity board director has been found to add as much as 3% to a company's stock price.[2]

Leadership

➤ A board director's leadership skill is essential for holding a governance position at a company.

➤ Leadership is the ability to influence, motivate, and enable others to contribute toward the effectiveness of the organizations of which they are members.

➤ Leadership and management are both stressful during times of economic downturns yet an opportunity for optimizing operations, and leaders do not necessary need to be in a formal leadership position to exert leadership behavior.

✓ A board director as leader must (a) involve the right people in the decision, at the right time, in the right way; (b) use a process that keeps people engaged and on track; (c) recognize the power of shared decision making; and (d) ask a series of key questions to avoid ineffective decision making.[3]

Celebrity Board Director

➤ A celebrity board director is an officer with significant influence in the company's governance decision-making process and who possesses one or more celebrity traits including credibility, goodwill, rights, image, influence, liability, and standard of value. A board director's leadership and decision making affects the governance and wealth maximization of shareholders' wealth.

✓ When a leader is considering what constitutes shareholder value; the leader should also consider that in practice the value proposition might not hold up given the gap between the stakeholder expectation and the realities of fulfilling that expectation.[4]

A question remains whether the perception of a celebrity board director is a universal phenomenon or specific to boards within the United States. Researchers suggest that "the value of high-profile board members is starting to be determined more in terms of leadership or expertise in a particular area than in their public notoriety."[5] A definition for celebrity is a famous person or a person who is widely known in society and business who commands a degree of public and media attention.[6] Phenomenon of celebrity seems to indicate that celebrity requires not only fame but also fame with an evident monetary value.[7]

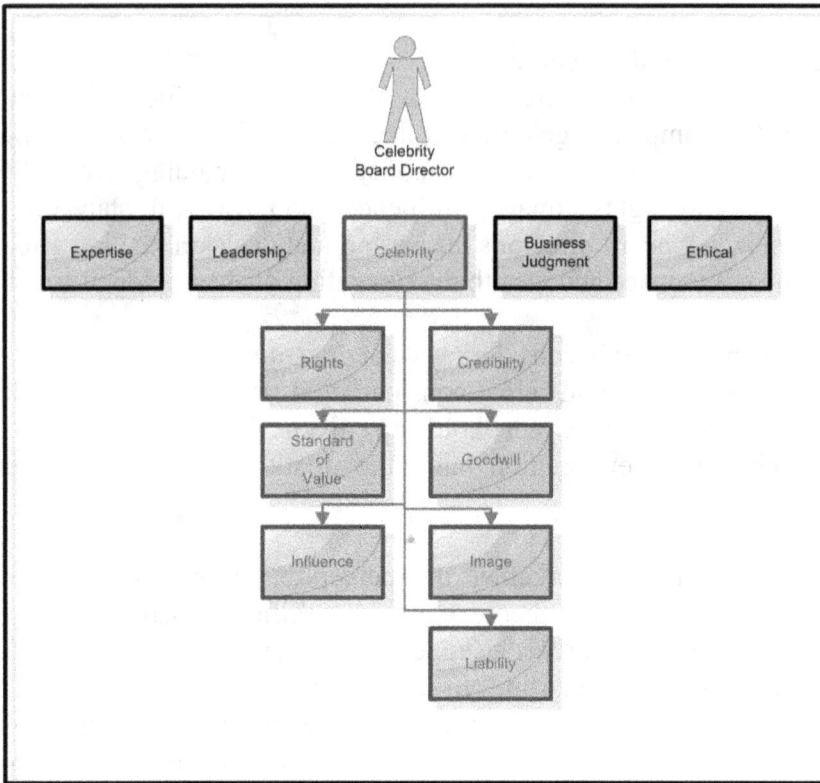

Figure 6-Celebrity Board Director Characteristics

In the case of a celebrity board director and corporate governance practice, the shareholders' wealth potential is at stake. Clearly defined in U.S. business law, a board is a corporation's ultimate authority.[8] Effective corporate governance requires leadership in addition to influence. Many U.S. companies have long stocked the company's board with a number of influential board directors.[9]

A company's leadership expects the celebrity component of a celebrity board director to bring perceived value, press, and investor interest.[10] Board Director is an officer with significant influence in a company's governance decision making who is charged with impeccable credentials as an agent on behalf of the shareholders.[11] However, according to researchers "The SEC, for its part, is considering a series of rules that would call into question the relevant qualifications of certain celebrity directors that have found a place on public company boards."[12]

Celebrity Board Director or Not

➢ Researchers found in 2011 at the impact of more than 700 celebrity directors that a celebrity board director may raise a business' visibility among consumers, investors and even analysts as well as the stock price on average by as much as 3 percentage points over a year.[13]

➢ Celebrity status includes celebrity, credibility, goodwill, rights, standard of value, directorship, image, influence, as well as celebrity liability.

Celebrity Credibility

➢ Celebrity credibility represents a situation in which an individual has been elevated to the level of a celebrity.[14]

➢ Elevated level of celebrity is due to a person's degree of recognition from others and distinctive qualities unique from others.

Celebrity Goodwill

➢ Celebrity goodwill reflects a number of factors including age, health, past earning power, reputation, skill, comparative success, and length of time in business.[15]

Celebrity Rights

➢ A person with celebrity status and associated rights where specific, identifiable, and tangible assets or items of intellectual property relate to a person's celebrity status.[16]

Celebrity Standard of Value

➢ Represents a measure of celebrity goodwill. Celebrity goodwill can be associated with a celebrity's image and influence can be expressed through a celebrity's endorsement, a celebrity's credibility, or a celebrity's goodwill.[17]

➢ Researchers observed most often celebrity appointments are made by boards of directors from large, profitable businesses with higher than average valuations.[18]

Celebrity Image, Celebrity Influence, and Celebrity Liability

➢ A celebrity is an individual who represents symbolic icons popular in a culture and transfers his or her symbolic meaning to the product endorsements and services offered by a person with celebrity goodwill. Researchers suggest that "Generally speaking, celebrity directors endow companies with sudden prominence, name recognition, some glamour, and, in many cases, a short-term spike in the stock price."[19]

✓ A person with celebrity goodwill casts images that influence product images when the celebrity is associated with the product through product endorsements.

✓ Likewise, a person with celebrity goodwill has been known both to possess the ability and to communicate distinctive bundles of various meanings or images, kinds of images or meanings.

✓ However, the root cause for the underlying causal effect of celebrity is unknown.

✓ A liability can be attributed to celebrity status to specific identifiable tangible assets or items of intellectual property.

✓ Celebrity liability takes the form of intrusion into personal affairs from publicity. For example, celebrity liability might occur if a celebrity board director dines at a restaurant with his or her family and is overheard making comments about leadership problems at the company where he or she holds a board position.

Other Celebrity Board Director Characteristics

➢ Other characteristics of a celebrity board director include ethical, solid business judgment, reliable agent, informed stakeholder, and effective stewardship.

➢ Business ethics is important not only to the overall effectiveness of corporate governance in place at a company but also to the person who holds the board director's position because business ethics reflects the board director's judgment and decision-making abilities.

   ✓ Corporate failures such as Enron's as well as economic conditions have resulted in increased regulation and legislation.[20]

   ✓ Each member of the board must take his or her position on the board seriously and apply due diligence during the decision-making process.

   ✓ A lack of ethical judgment in the decision-making process can erode the governance and also possibly lead to poor stewardship on behalf of the stakeholder.

   ✓ The virtue ethics model supports corporate governance with the idea of creating the greatest good for the overall stakeholder collective.[21]

   ✓ Each board member must demonstrate trustworthiness and virtue as well as act in good faith as an agent on behalf of all company stakeholders.

➢ Effective corporate governance ability and legal compliance are intertwined, and each board member must be familiar with the legal consequence of his or her decision making as part of the company's governance body.

   ✓ Two primary legal aspects of governance that a board director must pay attention are the Sarbanes-Oxley Act and business judgment rule.[22]

   ✓ The Sarbanes-Oxley Act of 2002 addresses financial stewardship concerns by shareholders with a company's leadership.

   ✓ Like the Sarbanes-Oxley Act, the business judgment rule is useful when members of the board come under scrutiny from upset shareholders.

   ✓ The business judgment rule is a good faith effort to obtain information to avoid class-action lawsuits by shareholders.[23]

➢ Each member of the board must be familiar with the consequences of not acting in the best interest of the shareholders.[24]

  ✓ Agency theory provides the framework for a board member's behavior that aligns with effective corporate governance.
  ✓ In agency theory and corporate governance, self-interested board directors appropriate value to themselves.
  ✓ The traditional perspective on corporate governance includes agency and stakeholder theories.

➢ The stakeholder theory is as important as agency theory. Each member of the board must be familiar with the consequences of his or her actions given the competing interest of both internal and external stakeholders with interests in the company.

  ✓ Without familiarity of stakeholder theory, the board member is less than prepared to contribute to an effective governance body.
  ✓ With stakeholder theory the existence of a complex bargaining process involves multiple interests.[25]
  ✓ The multiple competing interests can be found at each level of management within a company, starting at the top with the board of directors.
  ✓ A stakeholder board may be less efficient at generating total benefits.[26]
  ✓ The stakeholder theory defines different groups of interest represented by stakeholders where stakeholders have competing interests yet the desire for the same end, which is to receive some type of benefit.

> Stewardship theory is another building block that provides a foundation for an effective governance body.

  ✓ In stewardship theory and corporate governance, board directors maximize value for the company where the allocation of the board is by shareholders in agency theory and by managers in stewardship theory.[27]
  ✓ According to stewardship theory applied to corporate governance, a board director is an agent on behalf of the stakeholder.
  ✓ The board director's motivation essentially is to do a good job with managing corporate assets as a good steward.

Monetizing Celebrity

> Researchers noted that a person perceived to be a celebrity is different from other people through both monetary and status distinctions.[28] A person with a board director's title who sits on a board of directors for a company can be considered a celebrity board director with both monetary and celebrity status distinctions. A monetary definition of celebrity is possible when a person's earnings capacity increases with his or her celebrity.[29]

> The emotional responses, mostly positive, that define celebrity translate into an increase in the economic opportunities available to a company from the high level of public attention.[30] Simply put a celebrity translates into free advertising for a business.[31] For example, an investment or intrinsic value can be placed on professional goodwill. In this case, the valuation techniques that look at the value of the professional as distinguished from rights associated with the entity operated by the professional. The value of the holder of celebrity requires not only fame but also fame with an evident monetary value.[32]

ENDNOTES

1. Ambrose (2013).
2. Scott (2010).
3. Schwarber (2005).
4. Chowdhury (2003), p. 140.
5. Scott (2010), p. 1.
6. InsFishman et al. (2003).
7. Rein et al. (2005).
8. Tan, Fischer, Mitchell, and Phan (2009).
9. See "Buffett blames boardroom apathy" (2003).
10. Marshal (2006).
11. Arjoon (2006).
12. Corcoran (2010), para. 5.
13. Ambrose (2013).
14. Goldsmith et al. (2000).
15. Rounick and Riggs (2001).
16. Rosenthal et al. (2007).
17. Langmeyer and Walker (1991).
18. Ferris, Kim, Nishikawa and Unlu (2011).
19. Ghosh (2011), p. 1.
20. Rothschild (2002).
21. Caldwell and Ranjan (2005).
22. Creech (2006).
23. Hall and Lieberman (1998).
24. Dobson (2005).
25. Morgan (1994).
26. Williamson and Bercovitz (1994).
27. Turnbull (1997).
28. Rojek (2004).
29. Turner, (2006).
30. Rindova et al. (2006).
31. DiManno (2013).
32. Rein et al. (2005).

REFERENCES

Ambrose, E. (2013, July 14). Celebrities on the corporate board. *The Baltimore Sun.*

Arjoon, S. (2006). Striking a balance between rules and principles-based approaches for effective governance: A risks-based approach. *Journal of Business Ethics,* 68(1), 53.

"Buffett blames boardroom apathy" (2003). *Investor Relations Business,* 8(6), 7-8.

Caldwell, C., Ranjan, K. (2005). Organizational governance and ethical systems: A covenantal approach to building trust. *Journal of Business Ethics,* 2(58), 249–259.

Chowdhury, S. (2003). *Organization 21C: Someday all organizations will lead this way.* Upper Saddle River, N.J.: Prentice Hall.

Corcoran, G. (2010). The human victory cigar: Corporate edition. *The Wall Street Journal.* Retrieved on March 23, 2010 from http://blogs.wsj.com/deals/2010/03/23/the-human-victory-cigar-corporate-edition

Creech, D. (2006). Sarbanes-Oxley and Cost Engineering. *Cost Engineering,* 48(7), 8–12.

DiManno, R. (2013, Aug 17). Celebrity senator was for sale to big business. *Toronto Star.*

Dobson, J. (2005). Method to their madness: Justifying managers' pursuit of growth, even at the expense of shareholder value. Treasury Affairs, *1(3), 26-32.*

Ferris, S. P., Kim, K. A., Nishikawa, T., & Unlu, E. (2011). Reaching for the stars: The appointment of celebrities to corporate boards. *International Review of Economics, 58*(4), 337-358.

Ghosh, P. (2011). Apple and Al Gore: Why are celebrities put on corporate boards? *International Business Times*.

Goldsmith, R., Lafferty, B. Newell, S. (2000). The impact of corporate credibility and celebrity credibility on consumer reaction to advertisements and brands, *Journal of Advertising*, 29(3), 43-55.

Hall, B., and Liebman, J. (1998), Are CEOs really paid like bureaucrats? *The Quarterly Journal of Economics*, 103, 653-80.

InsFishman, J. E., Feder, R., Waltrich, C., and Fishman, J. (2003). Celebrity as a business and its role in matrimonial cases. *American Journal of Family Law*, 17(4), 203-211.

Langmeyer, L., Walker, M. (1991). Assessing the effects of celebrity endorsers: Preliminary findings. In R. R. Holman (Ed.), *Proceedings of the American Academy of Advertising*, 32-42.

Marshall, D. (2006). *Celebrity and power: Fame in contemporary culture*. Minneapolis, MN: University of Minneapolis Press.

Morgan, T. (1994). *Untying the knot of war: A bargaining theory of international crises*. Ann Arbor: University of Michigan Press.

Tan, J., Fischer, E., Mitchell, R., Phan, P. (2009). At the center of the action: Innovation and technology strategy research in the small business setting. *Journal of Small Business Management*, 47(3), 233-262.

Rein, I., Kotler, P., Stoller, M. (2005). *High visibility: The making and marketing of professionals into celebrities*. New York: McGraw-Hill.

Rindova, V., T. Pollock, and M. Hayward. 2006. Celebrity corporation's: The social construction of market popularity. *Academy of Management Review*, 31(1),50–71.

Rojek, C. (2004). *Celebrity*. London: Reaktion.

Rosenthal, L., Donoho, C., Eskew, R., and Diamond, P. (2007). Celebrity rights of publicity: For sale, but not necessarily available for creditors. *Intellectual Property and Technology Law Journal*, 19(3), 7-10.

Rothschild, W. (2002). Where are the leaders? *Financial Executive*, 18(5), 26-32.

Rounick, J., Riggs, R. 2001. What's Perk-olating? How courts are handling perks, fringe, and other employment benefits. *Family Advocacy*, 23(3), 12-17.

Schwarber, P. (2005). Leaders and the decision-making process. *Management Decision* 43(7/8): 1086–1092.

Scott, M. (2010). Surprising celebrities on corporate boards, *Daily Finance*, 10(1), 1-2.

Turnbull, S., (1997). Stakeholder governance. *Corporate Governance*, 1(5): 11–23.

Turner, G. (2006). *Understanding celebrity*. Thousand Oaks, CA: Sage.

Williamson, O., Bercovitz, J. (1997). The modern corporation as an efficiency instrument: The comparative contracting perspective. In C. Kaysen (Ed.), *The American corporation today*. New York: Oxford University Press.

Chapter Five
Board Director's Effectiveness

> The subjects covered in Board Director's Effectiveness chapter include Board Directors' Colleges, Board Director Certification, Board Director Age, Overcommitted Board Director, Celebrity Board Director Influence, Legal Duties of the Board of Directors, Defining the Board's Role and Taking the Lead in Strategy Discussions.

A board director's ability to serve on the board of directors of a company is a tremendous honor as well as a tremendous responsibility. With this responsibility, the board director must seek ways to improve his or her skills as well as keep current on changes. However, changing times require assessment and re-assessment of governance practices and most board directors simply need a way to stay on top of the buzzword governance that is, the use of words that only have meaning to the people practicing and/or interested in the art of governance. Thus, attending a board directors' college is a very good way to take action.

A board director should become aware of his or her skills and abilities. The board director should seek to build both breadth and depth in governance in order to better his or her governance effectiveness associated with fulfilling the duties of the governance position.

Board Directors' Colleges
➢ Directors' College at Stanford Law School[1] is directed by distinguished faculty members of Stanford University's business and law schools. This program is ISS-accredited.
➢ Director's College at the University of Delaware—John L. Weinberg Center for Corporate Governance.[2]

Board Director Certification

➢ By imposing self-regulation, the company's board of directors can ensure each board director's responsibility to uphold the integrity of the board director's position in the areas, including agency theory, corporate governance, leadership, business ethics, and legal compliance. One way to support a self-regulation effort is by establishing a minimum competence bar with board director certification.

➢ A board director should become aware of certificate options available to help with keeping abreast of changes in governance associated with fulfilling the duties of the governance position.

Certificate of Directorship

➢ The National Association of Corporate Directors (NACD), a nonprofit organization serving the corporate governance needs of board directors and boards, provides a nationally recognized designation for corporate board directors.[3]

Board Director's Age

➢ A board director's age can be viewed as an important indicator of effective corporate governance.[4]

Overcommitted Board Director

➢ A board director's commitment to his or her position and the amount of time that requires due diligence in preparation for participating in making governance decisions can be viewed as an important indicator of effective corporate governance.
➢ A board director with too many other commitments might be less effective than a director who is less distracted with his or her involvement in other activities not associated with the position.[5]
➢ Board directors should look at themselves to determine if they are overcommitted and make adjustments in their schedule accordingly.

Board Director's Celebrity Influence

➤ A celebrity is famous or widely known in society and business. He or she commands a degree of public and media attention. Some synonyms of celebrity include hero, luminary, notable or personage. Interestingly, fame and celebrity does not mean the same thing.

➤ The phenomenon of celebrity suggests that celebrity requires a level of fame as well as fame with an evident monetary value. In the case of a celebrity board director and corporate governance practice, the shareholders' wealth potential is at stake.[6]

➤ A board director's celebrity influence can be viewed as a possible indicator of corporate governance performance. Researchers observed that emotional responses, mostly positive, that define celebrity translates into an increase in the economic opportunities that are available to a company from the high-level of public attention.[7]

Legal Duties of the Board of Directors

➤ Duty to monitor, duty of care, duty of loyalty.

➤ SOX and 404: requires CEO and CFO to certify that they have evaluated the effectiveness of the company's disclosure controls and procedures - will be audited in the future to insure compliance.

➤ Researchers found a significant increase in internal governance during the period when changes were imposed by SOX.[8]

➤ Duty of Care may be assessed individually

➤ Board directors with expertise may be held to a higher standard than other board directors

➤ Board directors are not insulated from liability by not voting on transaction or attending the relevant board meeting. Gesoff vs. IIC Industries, Inc.

➤ Business Judgment Rule: presumes that the standard of cares has been met.

Defining the Board's Role

➤ Board directors have limited time, limited knowledge, limited information and limited understanding of the "business". Governance is a group process. Yet boards must provide leadership in strategy and management succession.

➤ Board directors must agree with management on (1) Financial goals (2) strategic direction to achieve goals (3) plans for management development and succession. All this while assuring a present level of compliance. Operationally this means: Management develops and presents plans and the Board reviews, discusses/questions and eventually approves plans.

➤ Net: Management proposes - the board disposes. Board and Management should be a "team", each building on strengths:

➤ Board: Helicopter view, Limited Time, Broad experience, Objectivity.

➤ Management: Detailed knowledge, Full-time, Deep Involvement.

➤ Meetings are the primary place for boards to provide leadership. Board director group is assembled. Board directors as a group interact with management. The primary place where board directors learn and reach decisions.

➤ Important characteristics:

   ✓ What kind of information comes to the table from management? How board directors interact with management. The depth and honesty of discussion among board directors. How the board responds to conflict among themselves and with management.

Taking the Lead in Strategy Discussions

➤ Once the board and management have crafted explicit financial goals, they need to turn their attention to how the company will hit those targets. Specifically, the board directors must step back from fighting fires and consider how management's view of the future squares with their own broader, higher-altitude views.

➤ Board of Directors retreats provides good setting for this. The board and management should hold an annual two-to-three day retreat - uninterrupted time devoted to discussing the company's direction for the next several years. There is time for management and the board to interact, certainly, but time is also set aside for board director-only sessions, which encourage open and frank discussions and draw out knowledge and insights in an uninhibited way.

➢ Like Rome, new strategies are not built in a day. Research has found that shaping (or reshaping) strategies for the long term are a process that takes place over multitude board meetings.

ENDNOTES

1. See http://rockcenter.law.stanford.edufor more information.
2. See http://www.lerner.udel.edu/centers/weinberg for more information.
3. See http://www.nacdonline.org for more information.
4. Core, Holthausen and Larcker (1999).
5. Core, Holthausen and Larcker (1999); Fitch and White (2004).
6. Rein, Kotler and Stoller (2005).
7. Rindova, Pollock and Hayward (2006).
8. Baber, Liang and Zhu (2012).

REFERENCES

Baber, W. R., Liang, L., & Zhu, Z. (2012). Associations between internal and external corporate governance characteristics: Implications for investigating financial accounting restatements. *Accounting Horizons*, 26(2), 219-237.

Core, J. E., W.R. Holthausen, D. F. Larcker. (1999). Corporate Governance, Chief Executive Officer Compensation, and Company Performance. *Journal of Financial Economics,*51, 371–406.

Fich, E., White, L. (2004). *Ties that Bind.* Stern Business School, New York University.

Rein, I., Kotler, P., Stoller, M. (2005). *High visibility: The making and marketing of professionals into celebrities.* New York: McGraw-Hill.

Rindova, V., Pollock, T. Hayward, M. (2006). Celebrity corporation's: The social construction of market popularity. *Academy of Management Review,* 31(1), 50–71.

Chapter Six
Board of Directors' Committees

> The subjects covered in the Board of Directors' Committees chapter include Committee Types and Committee Action.

A board director should have a working understanding of committees. A board member is very likely to be either assigned to a committee or even head a committee during his or her tenure in a governance position. Committees are a way to formally draw together people of relevant expertise. They may have the advantage of widening viewpoints and sharing responsibilities (refer to figure 7).

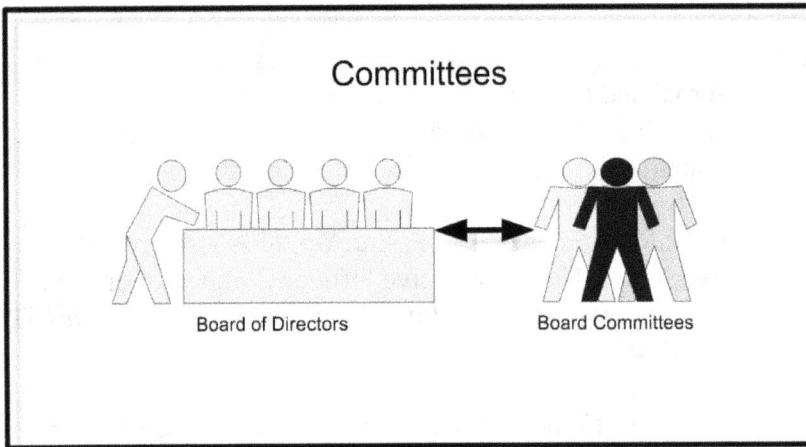

Figure 7-Board of Directors' Committees

Committee Types

➤ A number of different committees exist in the current corporate environment (refer to table 8).

Committee	Committee Functional Description
Audit Committee	❖ Assists the board in its oversight of the integrity of the financial statements; compliance with legal and regulatory requirements; compliance with ethical standards; and independence and performance of internal and independent auditors.
Compensation Committee	❖ Provides oversight and determination of executive compensation. ❖ Reviews and makes recommendations to the board about major compensation plans, policies, and programs of the company. ❖ Researchers observed that members of this particular committee seek balance among the views and needs from various stakeholders including management, shareholders, public observers, the media, regulators, and even themselves.[1]
Executive Committee	❖ Performs the duties and exercises the powers of the board of directors between regularly scheduled board meetings or when not practical or feasible for the board to meet.
Nominating Committee	❖ In conjunction with the executive committee, addresses issues such as needed expertise, background, leadership skills, willingness to participate actively, and inter-organizational relationships. ❖ Seeks to ensure overall diversity of representatives and balance of interests on the board where researchers found that

	the board is less likely to be independent when the CEO serves on the nomination committee.[2]
Finance Committee	❖ Assists the board in its oversight of the management of the organization's financial assets. ❖ Reviews and recommends approval of an annual operating budget. ❖ Regularly reviews financial results. ❖ Ensures the maintenance of an appropriate capital structure.
Pensions and Benefit Committee	❖ Assists the board in fulfilling its oversight responsibilities related to all company-sponsored savings or retirement plans. ❖ Reviews the financial administration of all plans. ❖ Advises on the proper management of plan assets and liabilities. ❖ Assists management in monitoring compliance with laws and regulations governing the management of plan assets.
Stock Option Committee	❖ Oversees the company's compensation policies and programs, including developing compensation policies, providing policy and benefit plan oversight, administering a company's various stock plans and the issuance of stock options and other stock-related awards not granted pursuant to a plan, and specifically addressing the compensation of the a company's executive officers.
Public Policy Committee	❖ Researches issues of public policy. ❖ Prepares position papers. ❖ Makes recommendations for action to the board. ❖ Ad hoc members of the public policy committee are typically added with board approval to achieve needed expertise on

	particular issues.
Investment Committee	❖ Develops an investment policy. ❖ Provides oversight on matters relating to investments made by a company.
Planning Committee	❖ Annually prepares a multiyear plan of the company's programs and activities. ❖ Recommends priority decision packages into the annual budget. ❖ Periodically reviews and reports to the board about longer-range plans, including determining when a new strategic plan needs development.
Human Resources Committee	❖ Reviews the employee needs for the company, the company's handbook, as well as salaries, wages and benefits of the respective employees.
Contributions Committee	❖ Reviews and provides advice to the board on a company's overall contributions objectives, policies, and programs.
Environmental Committee	❖ Assesses the effectiveness of environment programs and initiatives that support the company's environmental policy ❖ Advises the board on matters impacting corporate social responsibility and a company's public reputation.
Service and Technology Committee	❖ Oversees a company's significant technology and services initiatives.
Ethics Committee	❖ Monitors the ethical practices of a company. ❖ Serves as advocates for the ethical practices of the membership. ❖ Hears complaints and makes appropriate recommendations regarding violations of the company's bylaws and code of

	professional conduct to the Board.
Corporate Governance	❖ Oversees implementation of the corporate governance guidelines and principles. ❖ Regularly reviews the overall corporate governance and recommends improvements when necessary.
Corporate Responsibility Committee	❖ Assists the board and management in addressing a company's responsibilities as a global corporate citizen, including responsibilities to various stakeholders, such as shareholders, customers, employees, and the communities in which a company operates.

Table 8-Committees and Committee Descriptions

ENDNOTES

1. Hermanson, Tompkins, Veliyath, Ye (2012).
2. Creech (2006).

REFERENCES

Hermanson, D. R., Tompkins, J. G., Veliyath, R., Ye, Z. (2012). The Compensation Committee Process, *Contemporary Accounting Research,* 29(3), 666-709.

Creech, D. (2006). Sarbanes-Oxley and Cost Engineering. *Cost Engineering,* 48(7), 8–12.

Chapter Seven
Mentoring Board Directors

> The subjects covered in Mentoring Board Directors chapter include Common Practice, Board Director Mentoring Program, Board Director Commitment and Board Director Mentoring Effectiveness.

Mentoring a board director is about building governing skills, establishing governing programs and measuring program effectiveness in order to ensure a right fit for a governance board. No one size fits all approach. Mentoring requires leadership, knowledge, skill, experience, courage, and patience. High-impact governance requires on-going development of board member governing skills and requires a governing board commitment and must be put into practice.[1] Adapt to a level that makes sense, track success through feedback and refine through a continuous improvement plan.

Common Practice

➤ A common practice is for a more seasoned board director to mentor a new board director as the executive transitions into becoming a board director. This is especially the case when the executive has been a serial entrepreneur with experience developing white label products or services (refer to figure 8).

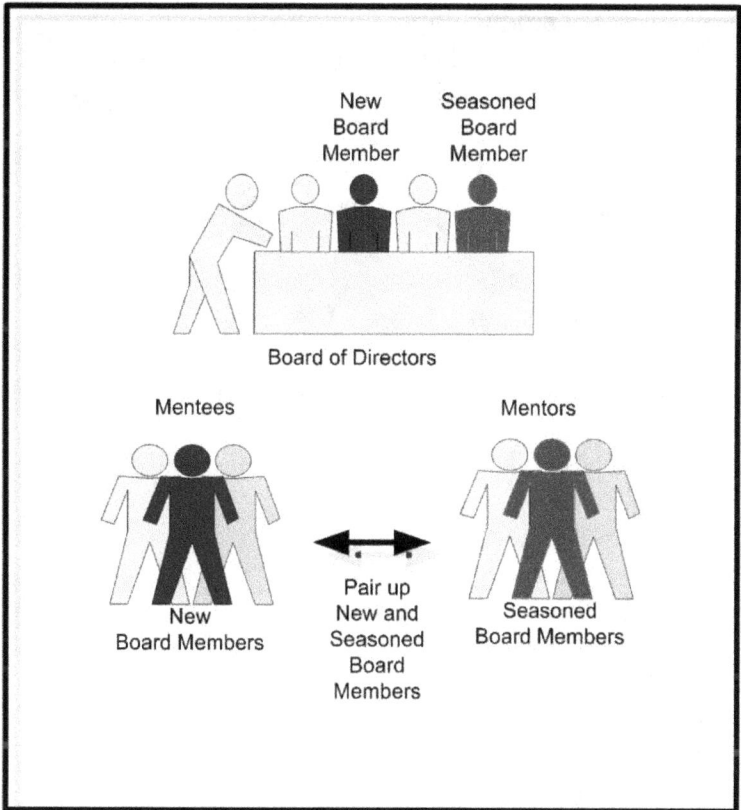

Figure 8 - Mentoring Board Directors

Board Director Mentoring Program

➢ Establishing the A Mentoring Program:
  ➢ Orientation.
  ➢ Mentorship.
  ➢ Continuing governance education and training.
  ➢ New Board Member Orientation Objectives:

    ✓ Minimize nonproductive time
    ✓ Understand the board's culture

➤ Incoming Board Member Mentorship Objectives:

- ✓ Increase productivity of new board member.
- ✓ Improve personal connections among the board
- ✓ Lessening the distance between newcomers and old hands.
- ✓ Contributing to a more cohesive board culture.
- ✓ Work through any interpersonal issues or problems that arise.

➤ Orientation Session

- ✓ In person (e.g. session outside of regular board meeting schedule).
- ✓ Media (e.g. DVD, Video).

➤ Orientation Binder

- ✓ Objectives of the organization.
- ✓ Board member role.
- ✓ Board member functions.
- ✓ Structure of the board.
- ✓ History of the board.
- ✓ The organization's "business".

➤ New Board Member Orientation

- ✓ Board member roster, including a biographical vignette providing professional and professional information about each member.
- ✓ Bylaws.
- ✓ The board governing mission statement.
- ✓ Board member performance standards.
- ✓ The standing committee structure, with detailed descript of each committee's functions.
- ✓ Guidelines for committee and full board operations dealing with agenda and report preparation.
- ✓ Board meeting and committee minutes/reports for prior six months or so.

- ➤ About the "business"

  - ✓ Values, vision, and missions statements.
  - ✓ Major milestones in the history of the organization.
  - ✓ Capsule descriptions of each major program/operating unit: goals, functions/services, staffing, budget.
  - ✓ Capsule descriptions of strategic change initiatives currently being pursued
  - ✓ The overall financial picture, showing major current sources of revenue, major cost categories, and revenue/expense lines – actual and projected.
  - ✓ The staff dimension, including the organizational structure, a roster of executive and managerial staff, and the number of staff per major category.
  - ✓ A map of service delivery sites or routes.
  - ✓ Information on conditions and trends in the field in which the nonprofit works.

- ➤ Incoming Board Member Mentorship.
- ➤ Mentee: Incoming board member.

  - ✓ Optional participation.
  - ✓ Required participation.

- ➤ Mentor: Senior board member should have spent a significant time on the board (e.g. typically at least two years):

  - ✓ Standing.
  - ✓ Rotational.
  - ✓ Required.

- ➤ Mentorship: Mentee assigned to a Mentor for a period six months or longer but depends on period of board member service.

Board Director Commitment
➢ Mentor commitment.
➢ Mentor plays an active role in orientation.
➢ Mentor meets with Mentee on regular basis outside of schedule board meetings (e.g. meet in person or on phone at least once or twice in between board meetings or as necessary).
➢ Mentor involvement.
➢ Standing mentorship – mentors assigned based on level of board attrition and incoming board members.
➢ Rotational mentorship – mentors assigned for a specific period but not necessarily for entire period of board service.
➢ Required mentorship – one or more mentorships required by all board members after a specific period of board service.
➢ Continuing Governance Education and Training.

➢ Governance Best Practices:

  ✓ Read periodicals, Wall Street Journal, and books on governance.
  ✓ Attend workshops and seminars on governance.
  ✓ Subscribe to an organization.

➢ Get involved with mentoring governance.

  ✓ Participate in a mentorship rotation based on the amount of commitment you feel conformable.

➢ Contrast and learn by joining two or more boards.

  ✓ Each governing board has something different to over its board members.

Board Director Mentoring Effectiveness

➤ Measuring Program Effectiveness.

➤ Track success through feedback.

    ✓ Survey incoming board members as part of interview process.
    ✓ Periodic surveys to existing board members.
    ✓ In person interviews by board chairperson.

➤ Refine through a continuous improvement plan.

    ✓ Determine right fit for board and board culture.
    ✓ Throw out what does not fit and add when gap presents itself.
    ✓ Use surveys to track improvement over time.

ENDNOTES

1. Eadie (2001).

REFERENCES

Eadie, D. (2001). *Extraordinary board leadership: The seven keys to high-impact governance.* Gaithersburg: Aspen Publishers.

Part II
Governance Performance

Chapter Eight
Organizational Models

> The subjects covered in Organizational Models chapter include
> Centralized Organizational Structure, Decentralized
> Organizational Structure, Federated Organizational Structure,
> Center of Excellence (COE), and Strategic Business Unit (SBU).

A board director's knowledge of organizational structures and
systems is a key to optimization of resources and maximization of
shareholder wealth. A board director should become familiar with
different organizational models that reused to structure the company.
Interestingly, companies tend to vacillate between a strong
centralization philosophy and a strong decentralization philosophy in
roughly three-year cycles.[1] An organizational structure and
associated culture reflects social factors, technology, and talented
individuals.[2]

Centralized Organizational Structure
> Centralized organizational structure reflects greater number of
> tiers to the organizational structure, narrow span of control, and a
> top-to-bottom flow of decision-effecting ideas (refer to figure 9).

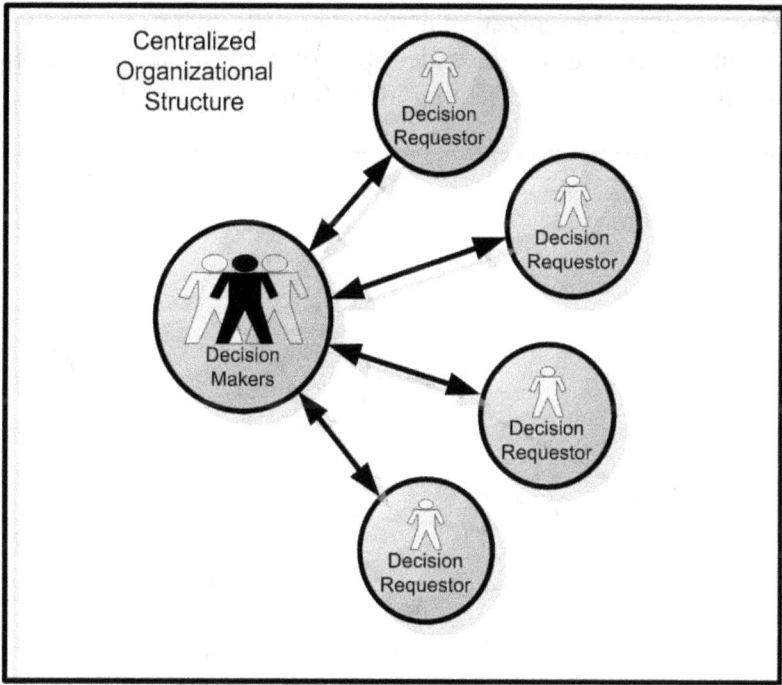

Figure 9-Centralized Organizational Structure

> ➢ Decentralized organizational structure reflects fewer tiers to the organizational structure, wider span of control, and a bottom-to-top flow of decision-effecting ideas (refer to figure 10).

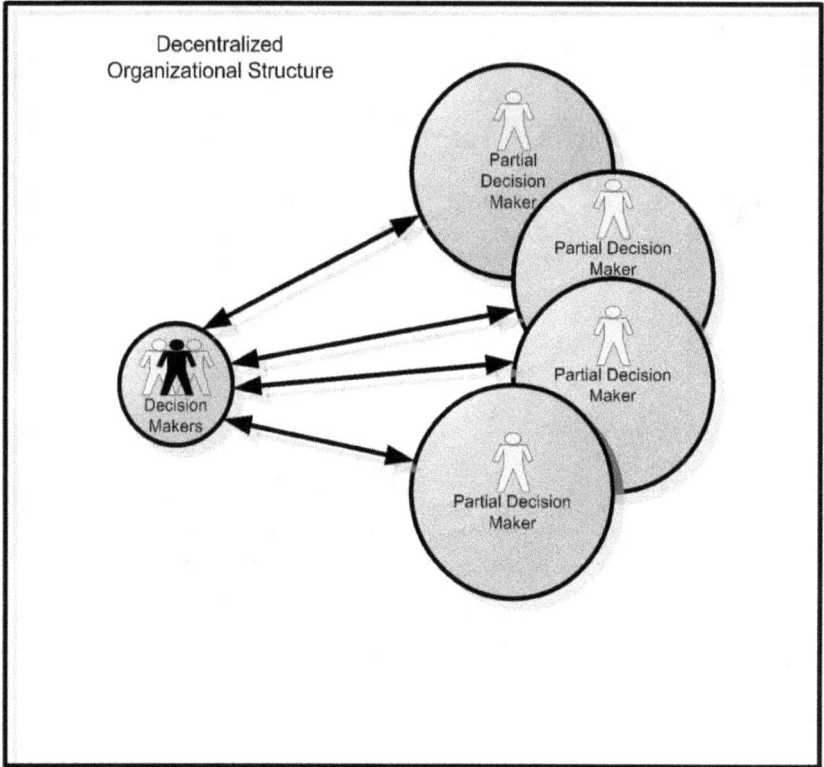

Figure 10 - Decentralized Organizational Structure

➢ Federated organizational structure reflects a hybrid structure between centralized and decentralized organizational structures (refer to figure 11).

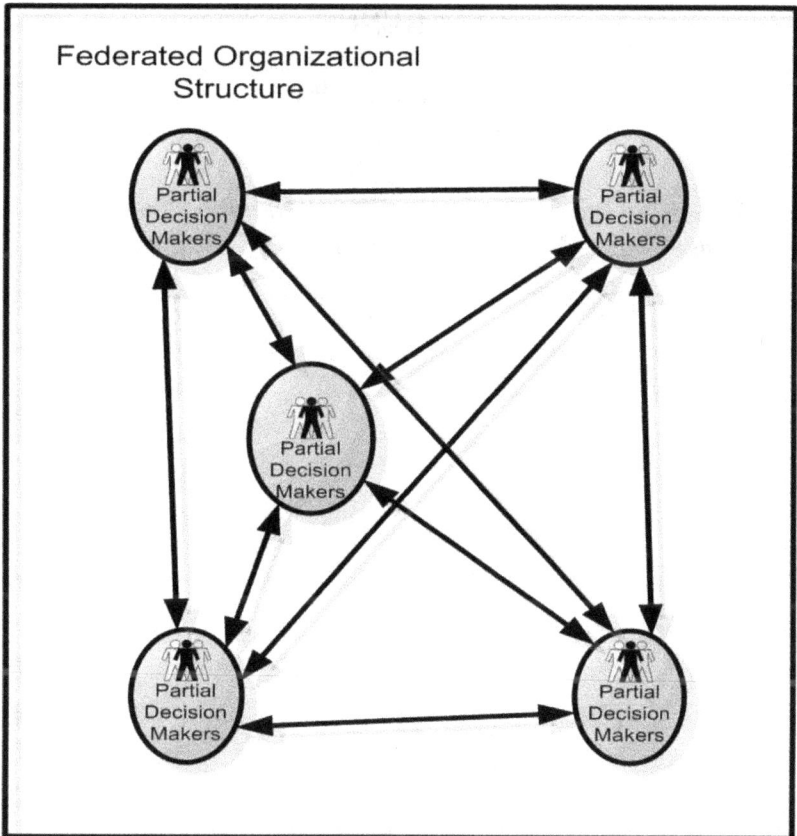

Figure 11 - Federated Organizational Structure

➢ A center of excellence (COE) is a formally or informally accepted body of knowledge and experience in a subject area. A COE consolidates expertise to maximize talent and productivity.
➢ A strategic business unit (SBU) can be found within the overall corporate identity. Once a company becomes really large, the company is best thought of as being composed of a number of businesses, or SBUs.

ENDNOTES

1. Ellis and Mauldin (2003).
2. Scott (2003).

REFERENCES

Ellis, J., T. Mauldin. (2003). Learning in the large enterprise: Centralized vs. decentralized. *Chief Learning Officer*.

Scott, W. R. (2002). *Organizations: Rational, natural, and open systems*. 5th ed. Upper Saddle River, N.J.: Prentice Hall.

Chapter Nine
Best Governance Practice

The subjects covered in the Best Governance Practice chapter include Governance Principles, Frequency of Meetings, Board Director Participation Checklist, SMAT Objectives Technique, KISS Technique, and SWOT Technique.

A board director should have a solid understanding of governance best practices in order to ensure his or her effectiveness in the governance position. Over the last few years, corporate governance has become an interesting subject with increasing pressure for both government and self-regulation, especially within the high-tech industry (refer to figure 12). Laws provide more transparency.

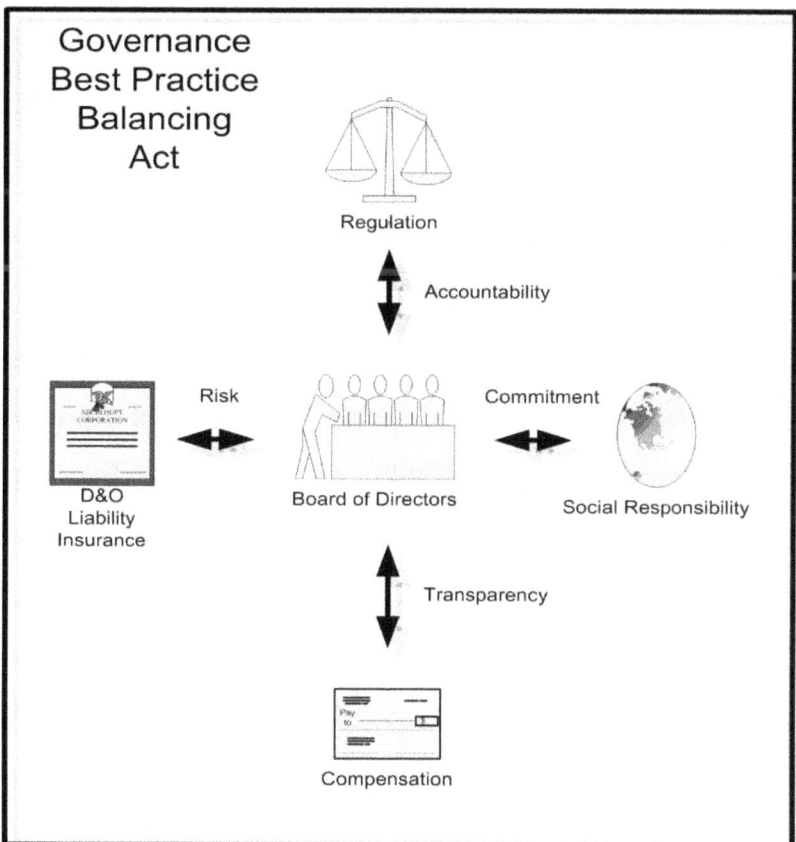

Figure 12-Governance Best Practice Equilibrium

Researchers found that there are five common principles that demonstrate good governance practice including 1) accountability, 2) efficiency and effectiveness, 3) openness and transparency, 4) participation, and 5) rule of law. However, there still remains some confusion that surrounds the concept of good governance practice.[1]

Shareholder advocacy provides oversight to ensure the board is acting correctly on behalf of the shareholder. First, the United States Congress enacted the Sarbanes-Oxley Act of 2002 (SOX) and equipped the Securities and Exchange Commission (SEC) to enforce and address financial stewardship concerns by shareholders with a company's leadership.[2] Second, the business judgment rule is a good faith effort to obtain information to avoid class action lawsuits by shareholders.[3] Interestingly, the business judgment rule has important influence with class action lawsuits and the corporate board of directors.

There is more detailed information about Sarbanes-Oxley and the business judgment rule in the chapter on compliance.

Governance Principles
➢ A set of principles or guidelines to be used by each person holding a governance position include rights and equitable treatment of shareholders, interest of other stakeholders, role and responsibilities of the board, integrity and ethical behavior, and disclosure and transparency.

Frequency of Governance Meetings
➢ Researchers observed that an increase in meeting frequency led to an increase in profitability.[4]

Board Director Participation Checklist

➤ A checklist helps the board director stay focused on the task at hand, that is, to ensure the board director has all the necessary data to make an informed decision. A checklist should include:

✓ Attend board meetings.
✓ Attend committee meetings.
✓ Read board reports prior to meetings.
✓ Advise and counsel the CEO outside of board meetings.
✓ Periodically formally evaluate the CEO's performance.
✓ Discuss management succession planning.
✓ Request specific information not normally included in board reports.
✓ Determine or request specific board agenda subjects.
✓ Determine or request committee agenda subjects.
✓ Direct internal audit activities.
✓ Direct corporate compliance activities.

➤ The board director could ask discerning questions during board or committee meetings about:

✓ Financial results and reasons for variances.
✓ Operating results and reasons for variances.
✓ Company strategy or its business model.
✓ Proposed mergers or acquisitions.
✓ Operating budget priorities.
✓ Capital budget priorities.
✓ Internal control strengths and weaknesses.
✓ Regulatory compliance.
✓ Legal issues.
✓ Personnel issues.
✓ Corporate culture and ethical conduct.

SWOT Technique

➤ The situation decomposition analysis technique uses the strengths, weakness, opportunities, and threats (SWOT) technique to gain a better understanding of the situation prior to making decisions. This technique helps the board director to assess expected internal and external factors, such as environmental, political, sociological, psychological, and fiscal changes.

➤ A board director should become aware of situation decomposition analysis in order to understand the importance of critical thinking skills associated with fulfilling the duties of the governance position.

➤ The internal and external controls ensure that decision-making transparency with the board of directors remains in effect (refer to table 10).

Internal Controls	External Controls
❖ Monitoring by the board of directors ❖ Remuneration (monetary payment for services rendered)	❖ Debt covenants ❖ External auditors ❖ Governance regulators ❖ Takeovers ❖ Competition ❖ Managerial labor market

Table 10 - Internal and External Controls

Making Boards More Effective

➤ A strong correlation exists between the failures of our major businesses (corporations) that can be related directly to our failures in the boardroom. For this reason, a board can take seven actions in the boardroom to help lead successful changes in their company.

➤ Strategic Planning: Let us get the board and management team working together on strategic planning. A board of directors' retreat is a great way to spend quality time together.

➤ Let us problem solve on a regular basis. If we were to do so, there would not be so many "over reactions".

➤ Information flow: Let's get the right kind of information to the board. For example, many of the board directors of our financial companies did not understand, let alone could they define "credit default swaps".

➤ Risk management is becoming as important as Audit, Comp., and Governance. Let us elevate risk management.

➤ All companies (whether public or private, profit or non-profit) should have board director education as a mandatory requirement.

➤ Executive compensation should be restructured to a longer term approach. An executive should also commit to a longer time frame in his or her role.

➤ There is a movement underway called "say on pay" in which companies must put non-binding shareholder votes on the annual meeting proxies. Board director's need to change executive pay before "say on pay" gains momentum and these currently non-binding shareholders votes becomes binding.

> ➢ Dissident shareholders are becoming more and more vocal and
> action oriented. Boards need to know their shareholders and
> keep them informed (specifically) about the company's long
> term strategy. A dissident shareholder is a person who opposes a
> corporation's management or management policy. For example,
> dissident shareholders of Hewlett-Packard opposed that
> corporation's offer to purchase Compaq Computer.

ENDNOTES

1. Doeveren (2011).
2. Creech (2006).
3. Hall (2004).
4. Yermack (1996).

REFERENCES

Creech, D. (2006). Sarbanes-Oxley and Cost Engineering. *Cost Engineering,* 48(7), 8–12.

Doeveren, V. (2011). Rethinking good governance: Identifying common principles. *Public Integrity*, 13(4), 301-318.

Hall, L. (2004). Can fairness opinions protect the board from liability? *Corporate Board,* 25(144), 22–25.

Yermack, D. (1996). Higher Market Valuation of Companies with a Small Board of Directors. *Journal of Financial Economic,* 40, 185–211.

Chapter Ten
Poor Governance Practice

> The subjects covered in the Poor Governance Practice chapter
> include Poor Governance, Breach of Duty and Corporate Crime.

A board director should become aware of poor governance practices in order to ensure that he or she avoids the pitfalls associated with fulfilling the duties of the governance position. The inability to self-regulate the code of conduct and business ethics for members of the board requires the government to impose regulations that will impact on the makeup and conduct of a company's board of directors, additionally these regulations influence governance standards of companies in countries outside the United States. For example, the Enron Corporation filed the largest dollar bankruptcy petition in the history of the United States on December 2, 2001 leading to considerable changes in law that impacted not only United States companies; but, companies all over the world.[1]

Poor Governance
- Poor governance is when the board of directors did not live up to the expectation of a company's stakeholders.
- Researchers observed that, when the situation comes to poor governance form, poorly performing companies with weak corporate governance in place and those board directors are more likely to be sued[2] (refer to table 11).

Company	History
Enron Corp.	❖ In 2005, ten board directors paid $13 million.
WorldCom Inc.	❖ In 2005, twelve board directors paid $24.8 million.
Trans Union Corp.	❖ In 1985, ten board directors paid $1.35 million. The case, known as Van Gorkom, spawned legislation limiting directory liability.[3]

Table 11-Examples of Weak Corporate Governance

Breach of Duty

➢ A breach of duty occurs when the officer of the company, as a reasonable person, fails to execute the duties of his or her position as an agent for the company and on behalf of the shareholders.
➢ Remedies for breach of duty potentially include injunction or declaration, damages or compensation, restoration of the company's property, rescission of the relevant contract, account of profits, or summary dismissal.

Corporate Crime

➢ White-collar crime occurs when an individual commits a crime while representing the interests of a corporation. These individuals may be employees, executives, or board directors.
➢ Typical crimes include antitrust violations, all types of fraud, environmental law violations, tax evasion, insider trading, bribery, counterfeiting, economic espionage, money laundering, and trade secret theft.
➢ Organized crime is where a criminal can set up a corporation either for the purposes of crime or as vehicle for laundering the proceeds of crime.
➢ State-corporate crime is the opportunity to commit crime emerges from a relationship between a corporation and the state.

ENDNOTES

1. "Eroding Confidence" (2002).
2. Brook and Rao (1994).
3. Lattman (2007).

REFERENCES

Brook, Y., Rao, R. (1994). Shareholder wealth effects of directors' liability limitation provisions. *Journal of Financial and Quantitative Analysis,* 29(3), 481–497.

"Eroding Confidence" (2002). *Business Week*, May 6, 2002.

Lattman, P. (2007). Settlement in Just for Feet Case May Fan Board Fears. *Wall Street Journal* 94, B6.

Chapter Eleven
Compliance

> The subjects covered in the Compliance chapter include Options Backdating, Sarbanes-Oxley (SOX), HIPPA, SAS 70, Business Judgment Rule, FCPA, and Patriot Act.

A board director should become aware of various compliances associated with fulfilling the duties of the governance position. There is no single approach with effective corporate governance that produces better-managed companies and satisfies stakeholders' objectives. However, common governance best practices and standards that establish overall responsibility for ethical and legal compliance, that align with long-term interests must start with the board of directors, regardless of the country in which the company resides.[1]

High-profile failures over the last few years have meant that there is greater attention paid to corporate leadership and governance. These failures led to the Sarbanes-Oxley Act of 2002. Other regulatory acts are the Health Insurance Portability and Accountability Act (HIPAA), Statement on Auditing Standard 70, business judgment rule, Foreign Corrupt Practices Act of 1977, and United States Patriot Act of 2001.

Options Backdating

➤ This is the practice of granting an employee stock option that is dated prior to the date that the company actually granted the option.

➤ This practice raises a number of legal and accounting issues. The practice of backdating itself is not illegal, nor is granting of discounted stock options.

  ✓ What are illegal and the improper disclosures, both in financial records and in filings with the United States Securities and Exchange Commission (SEC)?
  ✓
  ✓

✓ Most of the legal issues arising from backdating are a result of the grantor falsifying documents submitted to investors and regulators in an effort to conceal the backdating.

Sarbanes-Oxley Act of 2002

➢ The Securities and Exchange Commission (SEC) enforces Sarbanes-Oxley, which addresses the shareholder's financial stewardship concerns by demanding transparency with the decisions from a company's leadership.[2]

➢ The act contains a wide range of financial reporting standards for all American public company boards, management, and public accounting companies.[3]

➢ Sarbanes-Oxley (SOX) contains 11 sections, including:

✓ Public Company Accounting Oversight Board
✓ Auditor Independence
✓ Corporate Responsibility
✓ Enhanced Financial Disclosure
✓ Analysts Conflicts of Interest
✓ Commission Resources and Authority
✓ Studies and Reports
✓ Corporate and Criminal Fraud Accountability
✓ White collar Crime Penalty Enhancements
✓ Corporate Tax Returns
✓ Corporate Fraud and Accountability

➢ Sarbanes-Oxley requires the SEC to implement rulings on requirements to comply with the new law.

➢ If a board director unintentionally fails to comply with Sarbanes-Oxley, he or she faces fines of up to $1 million and may receive up to ten years in prison. Intentional infractions create up to $5 million in fines and twenty years in prison.

➢ Sarbanes-Oxley provides whistleblower protection

➢ There are two examples of international Sarbanes-Oxley equivalents. In Canada, the regulation instruments are 52-109 and 52-111. In the United Kingdom, the regulation in place is the Turnbull Guidance and Combined Code. However, other countries have not come as far as both Canada and the United Kingdom, thereby leaving those other countries with corporate governance structures that are vulnerable to financial reporting inequalities.

Health Insurance Portability and Accountability Act (HIPAA) of 1996

➢ HIPAA established national standards for electronic health care transactions and national identifiers for providers, health plans, and employers. HIPAA also addressed the security and privacy of health data (refer to table 12).

HIPAA (Type I)	❖ Represents health insurance coverage for workers and their families when workers change or when workers lose their jobs
HIPAA (Type II)	❖ Represents a set of national standards for electronic health care transactions and national identifiers for providers, health insurance plans, and employers

Table 12-HIPAA Types

Statement on Auditing Standard 70

➢ The Statement on Auditing Standard 70, by the American Institute of Certified Public Accountants (AICPA), defines the professional standards used by a service auditor to assess the internal controls of a service organization, such as an insurance or health care company, and issue a service auditor's report.

Business Judgment Rule

➢ Business judgment rule is a good faith effort to obtain information to avoid class action lawsuits by shareholders.[4] A board director loses the protection of the BJR if he or she violates fiduciary duties, that is, to take great care in considering all relevant material information reasonably available.

➢ Business judgment rule prevents the court system from engaging in a post hoc substantive review of business decision made by a board director.[5]

Foreign Corrupt Practices Act of 1977 (FCPA)
➢ The Foreign Corrupt Practices Act (FCPA) of 1977 is a federal law requiring all companies that publicly trade stock to maintain records that accurately and fairly represent the company's transactions. FCPA also requires any publicly traded company to have an adequate system of internal accounting controls.
➢ FCPA applies to public companies as well as all companies in the United States.

USA PATRIOT Act of 2001
➢ The Uniting and Strengthening America by Providing Appropriate Tools Required to Intercept and Obstruct Terrorism Act of 2001, known as the USA PATRIOT Act or Patriot Act, is an American law that supports the fight against terrorism.

ENDNOTES

1. Arjoon (2006).
2. Creech (2006).
3. Arjoon (2006).
4. Hall (2004).
5. Prahalad and Hamel (1990).

REFERENCES

Arjoon, S. (2006). Striking a balance between rules and principles-based approaches for effective governance: A risks-based approach. *Journal of Business Ethics,* 68(1), 53.

Creech, D. (2006). Sarbanes-Oxley and Cost Engineering. *Cost Engineering,* 48(7), 8–12.

Hall, L. (2004). Can fairness opinions protect the board from liability? *Corporate Board,* 25(144), 22–25.

Prahalad, C., Hamel, G. (1990). The core competence of the corporation, *Harvard Business Review*, 63(3), 79–91.

Chapter Twelve
Governance Measures

The subjects covered in the Governance Measures chapter include Shareholder Payout by Boards, CEO Payout by Boards, Board Director Payout, More on CEO Payout, Governance Metrics, and Governance Advisory Companies.

Measuring the effectiveness of governance is a challenging task. This chapter addresses how governance can be measured. Even though, individually, each board director has a unique contribution to give to the governance body, the board of directors acting as a whole might not effectively govern. How does the board director know if he or she is part of an effective governing body? One place to look is how external organizations are measuring effective governance.

A board director is an officer with significant influence in a company's governance decision making and is charged with impeccable credentials as an agent on behalf of the shareholder. Researchers observed that corporate leaders must be individuals of good character that produce the best corporate governance results.[1] Transformation influence significantly influences employees' attitudes and behaviors as well as shareholder perception. Each member of a company's board of directors collectively possesses the transformational influence that establishes the values-based climate through which ethical values, expectations with ethical conduct, and legal compliance.[2]

An important governance measure is board member compensation, because the amount of compensation relates to the likelihood of a person to join a company's board. A situation associated with agency theory can arise when a board director's self-interest overshadows the interest of the shareholders. The person is typically a person who has accumulated wealth and possibly celebrity status through ventures prior to joining the board. Any increase in wealth generated during a board director's tenure on a board of directors is a concern of the shareholders because the shareholders must not only evaluate the effectiveness of the governance body but also accountability of each of the board directors (refer to figure 13).

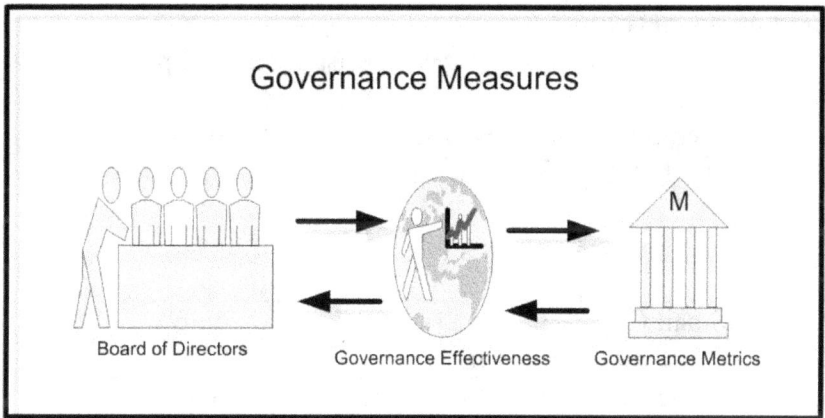

Figure 13-Governance Measures

A board director is typically compensated for his or her time spent on the board of directors. The compensation package varies for a board director and typically includes benefits, stock options, stock awards, paid travel, meal expenses, consulting fees, and salary.

Shareholder Payout by Boards
➤ Shareholders are concerned with their payout. A board director must ensure that he or she includes this concern in his or her decision-making process.
➤ When a board director is considering what constitutes shareholder value and whether in practice, value might not hold up, given the gap present between the stakeholder expectation and the realities of fulfilling that expectation.[3]

CEO Payout by Boards
➤ Researchers found that 1) board independence does not affect the level of CEO pay, 2) compensation committee independence causes CEO pay to increase, and 3) the increase in CEO pay occurs only in the presence of block holder board directors or high institutional ownership concentration, both of which are considered to be monitoring substitutes.[4]

Board Director's Payout (2013)

➢ According to a 2013 director compensation report published by compensation consultant Frederic W. Cook and Co., the board director compensation levels are largely dependent on company size (refer to table 13a).[5]

Company Revenues	Total Compensation
Small Cap (less than $1B)	$125,260
Mid Cap ($1B to $5B)	$182,500
Large Cap (greater than $5B)	$236,650

Table 13a - Total Compensation per Company Revenue

Board Director's Payout (2008 – 2012)

➢ In 2012, a board director's payout on average was $168,270 at a publically traded company (up nearly 30 percent from 2008).[6]

  ✓ In general, the increase in compensation reflects greater responsibilities and time commitments placed on board members.
  ✓ Board directors received less of their payout in cash (e.g. in 2008 the median equity component was $90,000 in contrast to the median equity component between 2012 and 2010 that increased to $107,415 from $100,000 respectively).

➢ Researchers observed that board director's payout increased to a record average of $251,000 for 250 hours of work in 2012 (sixth straight year of increased compensation since federal rules began requiring disclosure).[7]

  ✓ In 2012, board directors typically work 250 to 300 hours a year.
  ✓ Companies are required to report total compensation for board directors each year and provide breakdowns of fees, stock awards and other reimbursement.
  ✓ Proxy information provides transparency on payments for duties outside the boardroom including consultant fees or retirement income.

✓ According to a 2012 director compensation report published by compensation consultant Frederic W. Cook and Co., the board director compensation levels are largely dependent on company size (refer to table 13b).[8]

Company Revenues	Total Compensation
Small Cap (less than $1B)	$118,000
Mid Cap ($1B to $5B)	$178,000
Large Cap (greater than $5B)	$229,000

Table 13b - Total Compensation per Company Revenue

Board Director's Payout (2002 – 2007)

➢ In 2012, researchers observed that a board director's compensation averaged $152,000 per year in the largest two hundred companies and $116,000 per year for the largest one thousand companies.[9]

✓ The same researchers suggest that, when shareholders require information about the corporate compensation of the company, they are better able to evaluate the effectiveness of the board directors and hold them accountable for the salaries paid.[10]

✓ In contrast to CEO compensation, a board director is typically compensated for only his or her time spent on the board.

✓ The National Association of Corporate Directors (NACD) provided some insight into board director compensation as of 2007 (refer to table 13c). In addition, the referenced figures for total compensation are in line with 2006 research published by compensation consultant Frederic W. Cook and Co. based on 200 company public filings.[11]

Company Revenues	Total Compensation	Stock Option %
$50 - $500 million	$74,332	26
$500 million - $1 billion	$110,500	26
$1 billion - $2.5 billion	$132,760	29
$2.5 billion - $10 billion	$157, 165	21
Over $10 billion	$204,975	16

Table 13c - Total Compensation and Stock Option Payout per Company Revenue

More on CEO's Payout

➢ In 2006 equity's increasingly prominent role in executive compensation over the past decade resulted in substantial CEO equity holdings.[12]

➢ In 2002 researchers reported that median stock and option holdings of S&P 500 executives grew from $11 million in 1992 to more than $31 million in 1999.[13]

➢ Growth in equity holdings has been accompanied by a marked increase in sensitivity of executive wealth to stock price.

  ✓ For example, changes in CEO wealth from stock and option revaluations are over 50 times the wealth increases arising from salary and bonus changes.[14]

➢ Increased sensitivity of managers to stock prices has intensified incentives to manage earnings to maintain and increase stock valuations.[15]

➢ Although a substantial body of literature documents an association between capital markets concerns and earnings management, research into the role that equity compensation might play in this relation has only recently begun to emerge.

➢ CompensationStandards.com The Resource for Responsible Executive Compensation Practices is a "one stop" resource for information about responsible executive compensation practices.[16]

Governance Metrics

- ➢ Governance scores from governance advisory companies collect data on for-profit companies, so the board of directors' effectiveness and performance can be evaluated.
- ➢ Researchers have found that a causal relationship exists between stock market performance for a company, governance scores and company financial performance.[17]
- ➢ Evidence was found that suggests a positive relationship between a company's value and the quality of corporate governance.[18]
- ➢ The governance index (or G-index) provides insight into gauging governance effectiveness for a company's board of directors.
- ➢ Governance G-index is twenty-four governance provisions that have been classified into five categories of management power. A higher G-index indicates lower shareholder rights and weaker governance.
- ➢ The sixty-five factors of the governance score (G-score) also called the Corporate Governance Quotient (CGQ) represent either one or zero, depending on whether the company's governance standards are minimally acceptable.
- ➢ The sum of the fifty-one binary variables derives the G-score. The score represents twenty-three unique industry groups with 9 factors in common between G-score and the g-index that include blank check, bylaws, charter, classified board, cumulative voting, poison pill, special meeting, supermajority, written consent.
- ➢ Boardroom Metrics provides governance tools and management services to help improve the performance of business.[19]

Governance Advisory Companies

➢ MSCI.[20] (MSCI acquired RiskMetrics Group in 2010; RiskMetrics Group acquired Institutional Shareholder Services in 2007).

- ✓ Provides the Corporate Governance Quotient (CGQ) previously called the G-score
- ✓ Provides clarity on metrics. Founded in 1985, ISS is the world's leading provider of proxy voting and corporate governance solutions to the institutional marketplace.
- ✓ ISS defined twenty-three unique industry groups.
- ✓ Nine factors in common between G-score or CGQ and G-index include blank check, bylaws, charter, classified board, cumulative voting, poison pill, special meeting, supermajority, and written consent.
- ✓ Two main ratings for each company – a company's standing within its own industry group (as defined using the SIC codes) and a company's percentile within its index.
- ✓ CGQ ratings are in percentages on a scale of 0 (lowest) to 100.0 (highest).

> GovernanceMetrics International (GMI).[21]
  - ✓ A leading provider of corporate governance research and rating services worldwide.
  - ✓ An independent corporate governance research and rating agency.
  - ✓ GMI rating scale: calculates a rating on a scale of 1.0 (lowest) to 10.0 (highest).
  - ✓ GMI rating report includes a summary of the company's overall governance profile and commentary on each of the six research categories employed by GMI:

    - ❖ Board Accountability
    - ❖ Financial Disclosure and Internal Controls
    - ❖ Shareholder Rights
    - ❖ Executive Compensation
    - ❖ Market for Control and Ownership Base
    - ❖ Corporate Behavior and CSR Issues

  - ✓ The Corporate Library (Merged with GMI in 2010).

    - ❖ A leading independent source for U.S. and Canadian corporate governance and executive & director compensation information and analysis.
    - ❖ Provides the TCL Rating that reflects subjective judgment and expertise.
    - ❖ TCL rating scale: A to F where A- and B-rated companies do not exhibit significant risk in any of the four basic categories; C-rated companies exhibit risk in no more than one category; D-rated companies in two or more categories; and F-rated companies were either bankrupt, delisted from an exchange

✓ Audit Integrity (Merged with GMI in 2010).

  ❖ Audit Integrity was founded in 2002 to develop risk management tools based on a statistical analysis of corporate integrity.
  ❖ The rating is primarily focused on accounting practices.
  ❖ Accounting and Governance Risk (AGR) rating
  ❖ AGR rating scale: 0 to 100, corresponding to "Very Aggressive" (approximately 10% of all companies) to "Conservative" (approximately 15% of all companies).

➢ The Investor Responsibility Research Center (IRRC).[22]

  ✓ Provides the G-index.
  ✓ The findings of IRRC can be traced to a protest of the Vietnam War that triggered a rules change, enabling stockholders to vote for the first time on shareholder proposals with social connotations.
  ✓ The appearance of those social proposals provoked a need among institutional investors for unbiased, clear reporting on the underlying issues and led to the establishment of IRRC in 1972.

ENDNOTES

1. Bragues (2008).
2. Arjoon (2006).
3. Chowdhury (2003).
4. Guthrie, Sokolowsky, Wan (2012).
5. See
   http://www.fwcook.com/alert_letters/The_2013_Directors_C
   ompensation_Report.pdf for more information.
6. See
   http://www.bizjournals.com/sanjose/news/2013/09/12/board-
   of-directors-compensation-on-the.html.
7. Green, Suzuki (2013).
8. See
   http://www.fwcook.com/alert_letters/2012_Directors_Compe
   nsation_Report_Non-
   Employee_Director_Compensation_Across_Industries_and_S
   ize.pdf.
9. Bebchuk and Fried (2004).
10. Bebchuk and Fried (2004).
11. Graziano (2007).
12. Weber (2006).
13. Hall and Murphy (2002).
14. Hall and Liebman (1998).
15. Dechow and Skinner (2000).
16. See http://www.compensationstandards.com for more
    information.
17. Ertugrul and Hedge (2005); Gompers, Ishii, and Metrick
    (2003); Core, Holthausen, and Larcker (1999); Core, Guay,
    and Rusticus (2006).
18. Beiner et al. (2006).
19. See http://www.boardroommetrics.com for more information.
20. See http://www.msci.com for more information.
21. See http://www3.gmiratings.com/index.php for more
    information.
22. See http://www.irrcinstitute.org for more information.

REFERENCES

Arjoon, S. (2006). Striking a balance between rules and principles-based approaches for effective governance: A risks-based approach. *Journal of Business Ethics,* 68(1), 53.

Bebchuk, L., Fried., J. (2004). *Pay without performance: The unfulfilled promise of executive compensation.* Boston: Harvard University Press.

Beiner, S., Drobetz, W., Schmid, M. Zimmermann, H. (2006). An integrated framework for corporate governance and corporation valuation. *European Financial Management,* 12, 249–283.

Bragues, G. (2008). The ancients against the moderns: Focusing on the character of corporate leaders. *Journal of Business Ethics,* 78, 373-387.

Chowdhury, S. (2003). *Organization 21C: Someday all organizations will lead this way.* Upper Saddle River, N.J.: Prentice Hall.

Core, J. E., Holthausen, W.R., Larcker, D. F. (1999). Corporate Governance, Chief Executive Officer Compensation, and Company Performance. *Journal of Financial Economics,* 51, 371–406.

Core, J. E., Guay, W. R., Rusticus, T. O. (2006). Does weak governance cause weak stock returns? An examination of firm operating performance and investors' expectations. *The Journal of Finance,* 61(2), 655-687.

Dechow, P., Skinner, D. (2000), *Earnings management: Reconciling the views of accounting academics, practitioners and regulators.*

Ertugrul, M., Hedge, S. (2005). *Corporate Governance and Company Performance.* Financial Management Association.

Gompers, P., Ishii, J., Metrick, A. (2003). Corporate Governance and Equity Prices. *Quarterly Journal of Economics,* 118,107–155.

Graziano, C. 2007. Ask FERF about…board of directors' compensation. *Financial Executive, 23*(4), 57-58.

Green, J., Suzuki, H. (2013). Board director pay hits record $251,000 for 250 hours. Retrieved on May 29, 2013 from http://www.bloomberg.com/news/2013-05-30/board-director-pay-hits-record-251-000-for-250-hours.html.

Guthrie, K., Sokolowsky, J., & Wan, K. (2012). CEO Compensation and Board Structure Revisited. *Journal of Finance*, 67(3), 1149-1168.

Hall, B., and Liebman, J. (1998), Are CEOs really paid like bureaucrats? *The Quarterly Journal of Economics*, 103, 653-80.

Hall, B., and Murphy, K. (2002), Stock options for undiversified executives. *Journal of Accounting and Economics, 33*, 3-42.

Weber, M. (2006). Sensitivity of executive wealth to stock price, *Corporate Governance and Earnings Management, 5*, 321-353.

Chapter Thirteen
Risk Management

> The subjects covered in Risk Management chapter include Why Risk Needs Consideration, Managing Risk, Risk Components, Identifying Risk, Assessing Risk, Managing Risk, Risk Management Plan, Business Continuity Plan (BCP), Disaster Recovery Plan (DRP) and Risk Institute and Associations.

A board director should familiarize himself or herself with the company's risk management plan. The board director should understand various trade-offs associated with the governance decision-making process as part of fulfilling the duties of the governance position. Risk management is the human activity which integrates recognition of risk, risk assessment, developing strategies to manage risk, and mitigation of risk using managerial resources.

Researchers have found that organizations with weaker corporate governance are indeed riskier, suggesting.[1]

Considering Risk
➤ Loosely stated, Murphy's Law reflects a popular adage that whatever can go wrong will go wrong.
➤ Sod's Law states that if anything can go wrong, something will.
➤ Finagle's Law states that anything that can go wrong will go wrong at the worst possible moment.
➤ Parkinson's Law states that work expands to fill the time available for its completion.[2]

Risk Components
➤ Risk is a potential event that has a negative impact on a business
➤ Impact is the potential effect a risk may have
➤ Probability is the likelihood of the potential event or risk occurring
➤ Identify the risk, classify the risk, rate probability, rate impact and determine risk mitigation

Identifying Risk

➢ Estimate factors include likelihood, value, percent of risk mitigated and uncertainty

➢ Residual risk is the risk that remains even after a risk mitigation has been applied

➢ An outcome of the risk identification process is establishing the monitoring and reporting structure including designating what function the reports will serve, who is responsible for preparing the reports, and who reviews the reports.

Assessing Risk

➢ Risk assessment assigns a risk rating or score to each identified risk, useful in gauging the relative risk introduced and making comparative ratings later.

➢ Risk assessment measures the risk, the potential loss, and the probability that the loss will occur

➢ Risk measures take the form of either qualitative such as "high, medium and low" or quantitative such as dollars and formulas.

➢ Risk = (likelihood of a potential event) x (value or impact) − (percentage risk already mitigated + uncertainty)

➢ The risks must be monitored and then assessed on a regular basis (e.g. measure compliance, justify resource expenditure, and provide greater insight into business process)

➢ A key factor in the success of the risk assessment is having an effective sponsor

Managing Risk

➢ Once risks have been identified and assessed, all techniques to manage the risk fall into one or more of these four major categories (refer to figure 14).

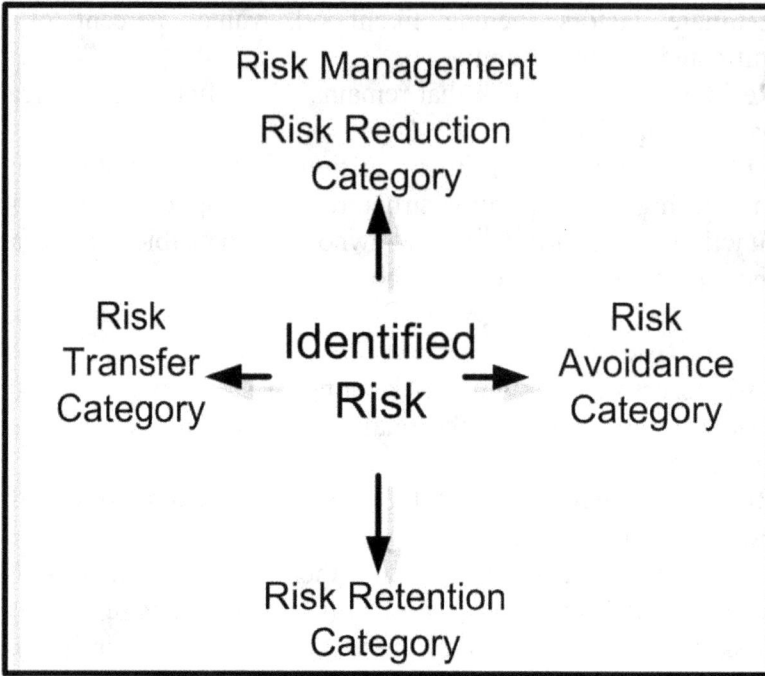

Figure 14 - Risk Management

- ➢ Risk avoidance may seem to be the answer to all risks, but avoiding risks also means losing out on the potential gain that accepting (retaining) the risk may have allowed.
- ➢ Risk reduction involves methods that reduce the severity of the loss, such as surveillance cameras to deter theft.
- ➢ Risk retention, a viable strategy for small risks where the cost of insuring against the risk would be greater over time than the total losses sustained, involves accepting the loss when risk occurs. All risks that are not avoided or transferred are retained by default.
- ➢ Risk transfer means causing another party to accept the risk, typically by contract or hedging. For example, insurance is one type of risk transfer that uses contracts.

Risk Management Plan
- The risk management plan should propose applicable and effective security controls for managing the risks.
- A good risk management plan should contain a schedule for control implementation and persons responsible for those actions.

Business Continuity Plan
- Developed by the company employees or consultants, a business continuity plan is a logistical plan that details how a company will recover and restore key business processes when an extended disruption in the business process or disaster occurs. A business continuity plan helps to reduce the operational risk and assess the amount of time to recover.

- Measurable business impact analysis and risk management are key tools that employees or consultants use to build and refine a business continuity plan.
- The business continuity plan lifecycle includes analysis, solution design, implementation, testing and acceptance, and maintenance.

Disaster Recovery Plan
- A part of the business continuity plan exercise, a disaster recovery plan details how to deal with unexpected or sudden loss of critical business operations. Possible events that constitute a disaster include terrorist attack, power failure, fire, theft, human error, equipment failure, and natural disasters.

Risk Institute and Associations
- The Institute of Risk Management.[3]
- Global Association of Risk Professionals.[4]
- The Fiduciary & Investment Risk Management Association.[5]

ENDNOTES

1. Brown and Caylor (2004).
2. Parkinson (1957).
3. See http://www.theirm.org for more information.
4. See http://www.garp.com for more information.
5. See http://www.thefirma.org for more information.

REFERENCES

Brown, L. Caylor, M. (2004). The Correlation Between Corporate Governance and Company Performance: Staff Reports, *Institutional Shareholder Services*, pp. 1-13.

Parkinson, C. (1957). *Parkinson's law*. Kuala Lumpur: University of Malaya.

Chapter Fourteen
Commitment to Quality

The subjects covered in the Commitment to Quality chapter include BPI Technique, Six-Sigma Technique, TQM Technique, Five Whys Technique, Cause and Effect Technique, Taguchi Technique, Community of Practice (CoP) and Institute and Associations.

A board director should become aware of key continuous quality improvement programs as part of building core competencies at a company to help to ensure competitive advantage. A board director should sponsor at least one quality improvement program as part of his or her commitment to quality in addition to the responsibility as part of the duties of a governance position.

Building core competencies allows a company to have a competitive advantage because the core competencies allow the company to offer its customers better value than competitors.[1]

Constraints and trade-offs associated with the decision-making process reflect a reality requiring leadership at all levels of the company; especially at the governance level (refer to figure 15).

Constraints and Trade-offs

Time
Constraint

50%

Trade-offs

Quality
Constraint

Trade-offs

50%

Scope
Constraint

Resource/
Costs
Constraint

Trade-offs

50%

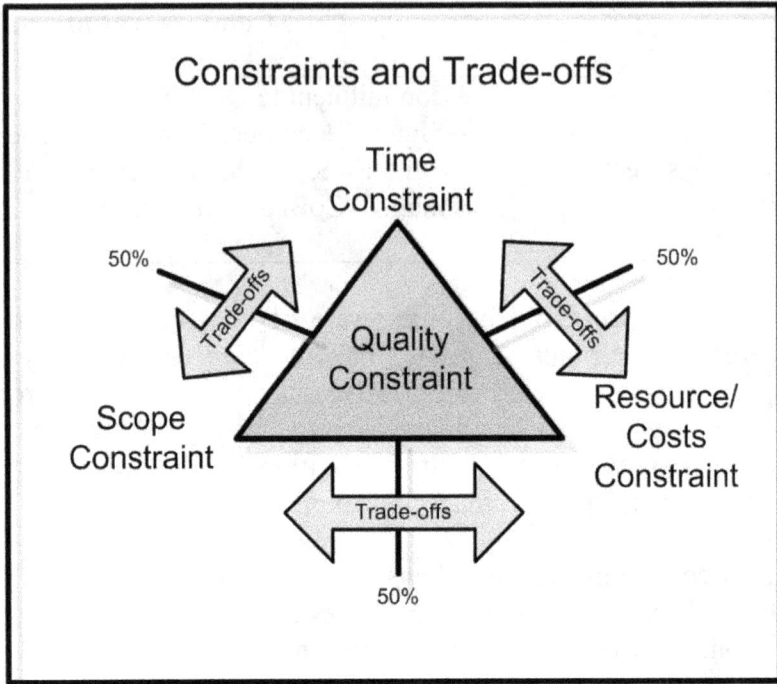

Figure 15-Constraints and Trade-offs

Business Process Improvement

➢ Developed by employees or a consultant, business process improvement is a systematic technique that helps any organization, including a for-profit business, a nonprofit organization, a government agency, or any other ongoing concern; make significant changes in the way the organization does business.

Six Sigma

➤ Originally developed by Motorola, Six Sigma is a system of practices that systematically improve processes by eliminating defects

➤ Six Sigma supports a number of key concepts (refer to table 14).

Critical to Quality	❖ Attributes most important to the customer
Defect	❖ Failing to deliver what the customer wants
Process Capability	❖ What your process can deliver
Variation	❖ What the customer sees and feels
Stable Operations	❖ Ensuring consistent, predictable processes to improve what the customer sees and feels
Design for Six Sigma	❖ Designing to meet customer needs and process capability

Table 14 - Key Concepts in Six Sigma

Total Quality Management (TQM)

➤ Total Quality Management (TQM), a management technique aimed at embedding awareness of quality in all organizational processes, has been widely applied to the following: manufacturing, education, government, and service industries.

Five Whys

➤ Originally developed by Sakichi Toyoda, the founder of Toyota, the five whys technique asks a series of "why" questions to explore the cause and effect relationships underlying a particular problem[2] (refer to table 15 for an example details the use of the five whys when a client is unhappy with a service).

1	Why	❖ We did not deliver our services on time to client.
2	Why	❖ The job took much longer than we expected.
3	Why	❖ We made a quick assessment of both time needed. We had an incomplete set of requirements necessary to complete the service.
4	Why	❖ We were running behind on other client engagements.
5	Why	❖ We have not had time to review both time estimation and requirements gathering procedures. This is the root cause.

Table 15-Five Whys

Cause and Effect

> ➤ Professor Kaoru Ishikawa created a cause and effect technique using a fishbone diagram, or cause and effect diagram that maps the cause and effect relationships.[3] Causes in a diagram are normally arranged in categories (refer to table 16).

6 Ms	Manufacturing	❖ Machine ❖ Method ❖ Materials ❖ Measurement ❖ Man ❖ Mother Nature (Environment)
8 Ps	Service Industry	❖ Price ❖ Promotion ❖ People ❖ Processes ❖ Place/Plant ❖ Policies ❖ Procedures ❖ Product (or Service)
4 Ss	Service Industry	❖ Surroundings ❖ Suppliers ❖ Systems ❖ Skills

Table 16-Cause and Effect Categories

Taguchi Technique

Genichi Taguchi developed the Taguchi technique to improve the quality of manufactured goods. This technique has been applied to biotechnology, marketing, and advertising.

> ➤ The cost of quality part of the technique is costs conformance and the cost of nonconformance to which the cost of innovation can be added.
> ➤ While the cost of conformance reflects the appraisal and preventive costs, the cost of nonconformance includes the costs of internal and external defects.

➢ Cost of conformance includes preventive and appraisal costs. Preventive cost is the cost incurred by the company to prevent nonconformance. The appraisal cost is the cost incurred while assessing, auditing, and inspecting products and procedures to conform products and services to specifications. Appraisal costs helps to detect quality-related failures.

➢ The cost of nonconformance reflects the cost of nonconformance, that is, the cost of having to rework products as well as the loss of customers that results from selling poor-quality products. Nonconformance represents costs due to internal and external failure.

Community of Practice (CoP)
➢ Groups of people performing similar roles
➢ Often in different groups and different parts of a business that interact based on common needs and concerns to share and increase knowledge

Institutes and Associations
➢ Chartered Quality Institute.[4]
➢ American Society for Quality.[5]
➢ National Association for Healthcare Quality.[6]

ENDNOTES

1. Afuah and Tucci (2003).
2. Ohno (1988).
3. Ishikawa (1985).
4. See http://www.thecqi.org for more information.
5. See http://www.asq.org for more information.
6. See http://www.nahq.org for more information.

REFERENCES

Afuah, A., Tucci, C. L. (2003). *Internet business models and strategies*. 2nd ed. New York: McGraw-Hill.

Ishikawa, K. (1985). *What is Total Quality Control*. New Jersey: Prentice-Hall.

Ohno, T. (1988). *Toyota production system: Beyond large-scale production*. New York City: Productivity Press.

Chapter Fifteen
Organizational Capability Maturity

> The subjects covered in Organizational Capability Maturity
> chapter include Learning Organization, Capability Maturity
> Model Integration (CMMI), Software Engineering Institute (SEI),
> Total Quality Management (TQM), and Pareto Principle-80/20
> Rule.

A board director should become aware of various capability maturity
models to help gauge the maturity of processes used within his or her
company. Sustained competitive advantage can be achieved through
consistent, repeatable business processes.

Executive management leads and establishes the culture and
consequent ability of an organization to capture, share, and manage
its knowledge. The culture of an organization is developed by the
structure, attitude, and example of management. An organizational
culture that integrates organizational learning concepts where both
action and reflection brings a richer set of perspectives that drives
better decision making within a company (refer to figure 16).[1]

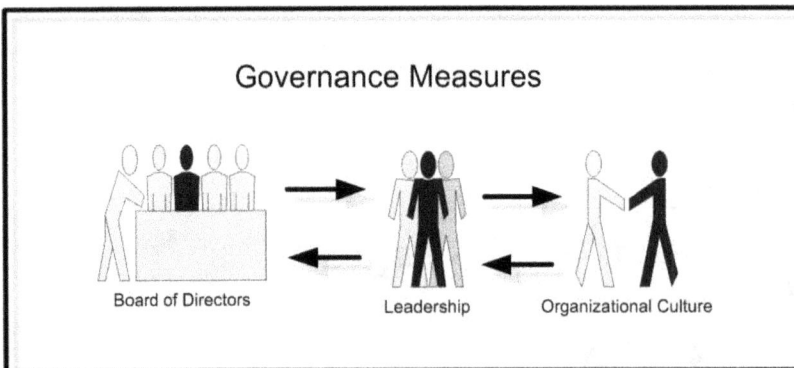

Figure 16 - Assessing Capability Maturity

Learning Organization
> ➢ Given globalization and the amount of information available via
> the Internet, a board director should consider building a learning
> organization capability to ensure competitive advantage.

> Researchers have found that a learning organization supports competitive advantage where the organizational memory requires capturing knowledge from previous situational events with associated decisions within the learning organization.[2]

Capability Maturity Model Integration (CMMI)
> Capability Maturity Model Integration (CMMI) helps organizations increase the maturity of their processes to improve longer-term business performance. CMMI provides the latest, best practices for product and service development, maintenance, and acquisition.

Total Quality Management (TQM)
> Total Quality Management (TQM) is a management strategy aimed at embedding awareness of quality in all organizational processes.

Pareto Principle (80-20 Rule)
> The Pareto Principle, or the 80-20 Rule, states that, for many phenomena, 80 percent of the consequences stem from 20 percent of the causes.[3] For example, 80 percent of a company's revenues come from 20 percent of a company's customers.

Institute and Associations
> Carnegie Mellon Software Engineering Institute (SEI) has served the nation as a federally funded research and development center.[4]
> Official ITIL Website.[5]

ENDNOTES

1. Senge (2006); Thomas (2003).
2. Senge (2006).
3. Messer (2007).
4. See http://www.sei.cmu.edu/cmmi for more information.
5. See http://www.itil-officialsite.com for more information.

REFERENCES

Messer, S. (2007). *Maximizing return from the 80-20 rule.* American Marketing Association.

Senge, P. (2006). *The fifth discipline: The art and Practice of the learning organization.* New York City: Random House.

Thomas, H. (2003). An integration of thoughts and knowledge management. *Decision Sciences*, 34(2), 189–196.

Chapter Sixteen
Business Value Rationalization Technique

> The subjects covered in the Business Valuation Rationalization Technique chapter include Total Cost of Ownership (TCO), One-time Costs, Recurring Costs, Project Duration, Return on Investment (ROI), Process Re-engineering, Risk Evaluation (what-if analysis) and In Practice.

A board director should understand the mechanics of the business value rationalization technique. There are three components to business value rationalization–total cost of ownership (TCO), return on investment (ROI) and risk evaluation (what-if analysis). The use of business value rationalization by a person helps to provide insight into a financial benefit/cost analysis. The board director should realize that, when making any decision that impacts the governance of a company, the initial step prior to making the decision requires determining benefit/cost trade-offs.

TCO Analysis
➢ Total Cost of Ownership (TCO) is a financial estimate analysis technique that is designed to help managers and board directors assess direct and indirect costs related making an investment (refer to figure 17).[1]

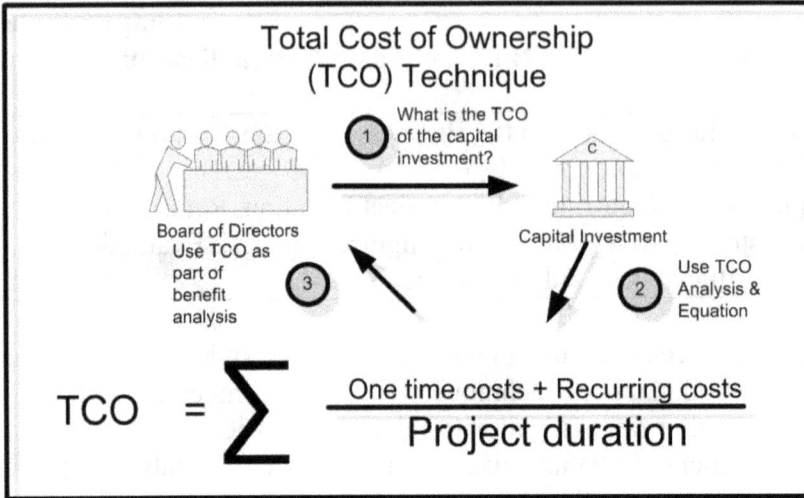

Figure 17 - Total Cost of Ownership (TCO) Analysis

✓ TCO provides a cost basis for determining the economic value of that investment.

✓ TCO includes the costs associated to the following: training personnel; failure or outage (planned and unplanned); diminished performance; security breaches or in loss of reputation and recovery; disaster preparedness and recovery; floor space; power consumption; development expenses; infrastructure; quality assurance (QA); incremental growth; and decommissioning.

✓ TCO should be reviewed along with other project benefit/cost calculations, including: net present value (NPV); return on investment (ROI); internal rate of return (IRR), and Economic Value Added (EVA).

One-time Costs

➢ One-time costs are usually incurred at the beginning of the project in the form of capital expense. They can also be incurred at the end of the project in the form of decommissioning costs to retire capital.

Recurring Costs

➢ Recurring costs are incurred periodically and originate from the maintenance, refurbishing of capital, and support of the initial capital investment.

Project Duration

> The project duration is the expected life span of the investment.
> Some companies standardize the project duration to one-and-a-half to three years, particularly for technology investments due to changes in technology.
> In contrast, other companies might not include project duration in the calculation, resulting in a TCO that reflects a summation of costs that are updated continually over the project's lifetime.

ROI Calculation

> Return on Investment (ROI) is the ratio of the business value gained or lost (whether realized or unrealized) on an investment relative to the amount of value invested. ROI is usually expressed as a percentage rather than a fraction. An ROI calculation combined with TCO to develop a business case for a given business value rationalization proposal.

> The formula for ROI is the final value (FV) minus the TCO divided by the TCO and multiplied by 100. That is, ROI is equal to [(FV- TCO) / TCO]*100. In general, when the ROI is greater than 0, the business value rationalization proposal should be accepted. Alternatively, when the ROI is less than 0, the business value rationalization proposal should not be accepted.

Risk Evaluation (What-if analysis)

> Risks which are not mitigated can often lead to an increase in project costs and a decrease in business benefit realization.

> ✓ As a result, the impact of risks should be modeled to create a business case.
> ✓ Used to assess the impacts of various risks, particularly on benefits.

Process Re-engineering

- ➢ Process Improvement can be achieved through business value rationalization

  - ✓ In today's business environment, the strongest competitors do more than respond to market changes — they anticipate them
  - ✓ But to forecast trends, an organization must work in concert toward the same goals, dovetailing their efforts for maximum speed and effectiveness
  - ✓ In the "do more with less" era of shrinking budgets and rising expectations, companies cannot afford anything less than top performance from the systems they choose
  - ✓ Board directors must develop a particular expertise in analyzing total cost of ownership (TCO) and return on investment (ROI)

In Practice

- ➢ For example let us consider a process re-engineering effort to increase business value proposal through a paradigm shift through the implementation of ITILv3 in order to transform the way help desk services are provided within an organization.[2]
- ➢ If the business value rationalization proposal is expected to produce a net gain of $1M (FV=$1M) in business value through a reduction in head count and with an initial investment of $0.5M (TCO=$0.5M) to implement a system and train personnel on the new system, the resulting calculation is [($1M-$0.5M)/$0.5M]*100 or 100 percent.
- ➢ So in this case, with a ROI is greater than 0 the business value rationalization proposal should be accepted. Do not forget to evaluate the risk (if any) associated with accepting the business value rationalization proposal.

ENDNOTES

1. David, Schuff, St Louis (2002).
2. See http://www.itil-officialsite.com for more information.

REFERENCES

David, J. S., Schuff, D., St Louis, R. (2002). Managing your total IT cost of ownership. *Communications of the ACM, 45*(1), 101-106.

Chapter Seventeen
Board of Directors' Business Intelligence

> The subjects covered in the Board of Directors' Business Intelligence chapter include Knowledge Asset, Knowledge Management, Knowledge Types, Knowledge Management System, Knowledge Management System Benefits, Knowledge Leadership, Corporate Memory, Competitive Advantage of Knowledge Management, Key Performance Indicators, Financial Performance Indicators Examples, Balanced Scorecard, and Board Communication Tools.

In order to make informed decisions associated with fulfilling the duties of the governance position, a board director should become aware of the usefulness of having access to business intelligence.

Business intelligence refers to skills, technologies, applications and practices used to help a business acquire a better understanding of its commercial context. Business intelligence may also refer to the collected information itself. Knowledge is increasingly seen as the most valuable asset of the modern organization.

A key challenge that is emerging for such organizations is how to encourage knowledge sharing. Increased realization of knowledge as the core competence, coupled with advances in information technology such as intranets and the World Wide Web, has increased organizational interest in the topic of knowledge management.[1]

Knowledge management efforts are typically focus on organizational objectives such as improved performance, competitive advantage, innovation, the sharing of lessons learned, and continuous improvement of the organization.

Knowledge Asset
> A company-specific resource that is indispensable to create values for the company.
> Includes the inputs, outputs, and moderating factors, of the knowledge-creating process.

Knowledge Management
➢ Comprises a range of practices used in an organization to identify, create, represent, distribute and enable adoption of insights and experiences.
➢ Such insights and experiences comprise knowledge, either embodied in individuals or embedded in organizational processes or practice.

Knowledge Types
➢ Tacit (knowing-how) knowledge: knowledge embedded in the human mind through experience and jobs
➢ Explicit (knowing-that) knowledge: knowledge codified and digitized in books, documents, reports, memos.

Knowledge Management System
➢ A system for managing knowledge in organizations, supporting creation, capture, storage and dissemination of information.
➢ The system consists of both people and computer systems.

Knowledge Management System Benefits
➢ Sharing of valuable organizational information.
➢ Can avoid re-inventing the wheel, reducing redundant work.
➢ May reduce training time for new employees
➢ Retention of Intellectual Property after the employee leaves if such knowledge can be codified.

Knowledge Leadership
➢ Knowledge Leaders are Leaders who are effective at…

✓ Embracing and driving change
✓ Sharing experiences and applying learning
✓ Modeling the expected behaviors grounded in the culture of the organization…in order to tap into the intellectual capital of the organization and harness intellectual capital to innovate and grow

Corporate Memory
➢ The justification for building an organizational or group memory comes from "if we only knew what we already know".
➢ There is huge leverage and competitive advantage to be had from capturing insights, recording proven solutions, preventing reinvention of the wheel, learning from errors and sharing experience.
➢ Intuitive navigation, individual tags, facile annotation and links to experts are the key affordances here.

Competitive Advantage of Knowledge Management
➢ Critical knowledge area can create a new perspective on the enterprise and how critical knowledge contributes value to an organization's customers
➢ Considered as a critical success factor and important for management decision making and the formation of competitive strategy
➢ The structure of an organization, its processes, systems, policies, and practices can be examined and adjusted to achieve greater leverage with the critical knowledge area.
➢ Some of these processes and systems include: acquisition/generation, store/retrieval, transfer, application, and protection

Achieving effective governance practice, in order to make sound governance decisions, board directors must have timely reports based on an aggregation of credible business intelligence data on the company (refer to figure 18).

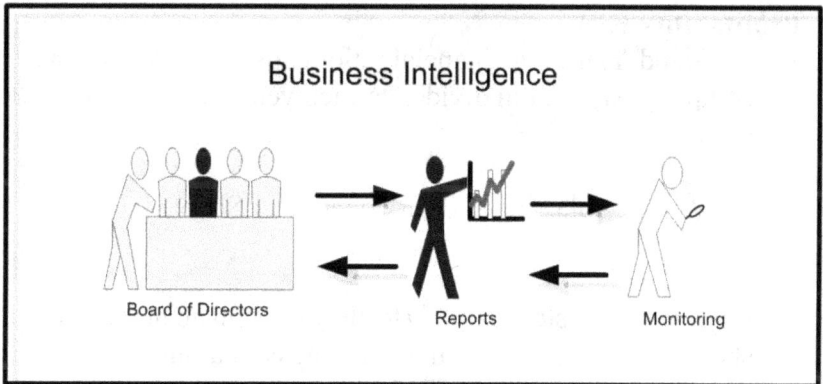

Figure 18 - Business Intelligence

Key Performance Indicators

➢ A Key Performance Indicator (KPI) is either a Financial or non-financial metric that used to quantify an objective that reflects strategic performance of an organization.

➢ A company must establish its strategic and operational objectives and then choose the KPI that best reflect those objectives. The timing of KPIs, relative to achievement of corporate goals, is fundamental in choosing good KPIs.

➢ KPIs are frequently used to value difficult to measure activities tied to an organization's strategy. KPIs should measure a continuous or discrete, but repeated, process.

➢ Financial and non-financial metrics are used to quantify objectives to reflect the strategic performance management of an organization. For example, a financial KPI might be to increase average revenue per customer or increase the gross profit margin. In contrast, a non-financial KPI might be to increase the number of customer sales prospects.

Financial Performance Indicators Examples
> ## Profitability KPI
>> ✓ Dividend Yield – A financial ratio that shows how much a company pays out in dividends each year relative to its share price.
>>
>>> ❖ Formula: (Annual Dividends Per Share) / (Price per Share)
>>
>> ✓ Return on Invested Capital (ROIC) – A financial ratio that shows the efficiency at allocating the capital under a company's control to profitable investments.
>>
>>> ❖ Formula: (Net Income – Dividends) / (Total capital)
>>
>> ✓ Return on Equity (ROE) – A financial ratio that shows the amount of net income returned as a percentage of shareholders equity.
>>
>>> ❖ Formula: (Net Income) / (Shareholder's Equity)
>>
>> ✓ Return on Investment (ROI) – A financial percentage or a ratio that shows the efficiency of an investment.
>>
>>> ❖ Formula: [(Gain from Investment) – (Cost of Investment)] / (Cost of Investment)
>>
>> ✓ Cash Flow Return on Investment (CFROI) – A valuation model that assumes the stock markets sets prices based on cash flow and not on corporate performance and earnings
>>
>>> ❖ Formula: (Cash Flow) / (Market Value of Capital Employed)

- ✓ Net Profit Margin – A financial ratio that shows a net profits to revenues for a company or business segment and expressed as a percentage

    - ❖ Formula: [(Revenue) – (COGS) – (Operating Expenses) – (Interest) – (Taxes) / (Revenue)]

- ✓ Earnings Before Interest, Taxes, Depreciation and Amortization (EBITDA) Margin – A ratio that measures the extent to which cash operating expenses use up revenue.

    - ❖ Formula: (EBITDA) / (Total Revenue)

- ✓ Sales Growth – The increase of sales over a specific period of time.
- ✓ Free Cash Flows to Sales

    - ❖ Formula: (Cash Flow) / (Total Revenue)

- ➢ **Valuation KPI**
  - ✓ Price to Book – A financial ratio that compares the market's valuation of a company to the value of the company.

    - ❖ Formula: (Stock's capitalization) / (Book Value)

  - ✓ Price to Cash Flow

    - ❖ Formula: (Market Value per Share) / (Cash Flow)

  - ✓ Price to Earnings is valuation ratio of a company's current share price compared to its per-share earnings.

    - ❖ Formula: (Market Value per Share) / (Earnings per Share)

> **Market KPI**
>   ✓ Total Shareholder Return (TSR) – represents the change in capital value of a listed/quoted company over the period (typically greater than a year), plus dividends, expressed as a plus or minus percentage of the opening value
>
>   ❖ Formula: (Equity Market Value at beginning of period – Equity Market Value at end of period + Dividends paid) / (Equity Market Value at beginning of period)
>
>   ✓ Tobin's Q - is a ratio comparing the market value of a company's stock with the value of a company's equity book value.
>
>   ❖ Formula: (Equity Market Value + Liabilities Book Value) / (Equity Book Value + Liabilities Book Value)

> **Risk KPI**
>   ✓ Volatility takes many forms – in this case volatility refers to the standard deviation of the continuously compounded returns of a financial instrument with a specific time horizon
>
>   ❖ Formula: (standard deviation of a stock's logarithmic returns) / (square root of the time period of the returns)
>
>   ✓ Z Score - may be used to predict the probability that a company will go into bankruptcy within two years
>
>   ❖ Formula: $Z = 1.2T1 + 1.4T2 + 3.3T3 + .6T4 + .999T5$ where
>
>   T1 = Working Capital / Total Assets
>   T2 = Retained Earnings / Total Assets
>   T3 = Earnings Before Interest and Taxes / Total Assets
>   T4 = Market Value of Equity / Total Liabilities
>   T5 = Sales/ Total Assets

Balanced Scorecard

➢ A balanced scorecard measures a company's activities in terms of its vision and strategies as well as gives the leader a comprehensive view of the performance of his or her business.

➢ A company's employees provide the input. The executive team uses a balanced scorecard to manage the business and present findings to the board.

Board Communication Tools

➢ Effective communication is the key to any type of relationship. One has to be careful about miscommunications and misunderstandings. Either of these factors often produces wasted time, hurt feelings, and negative outcomes. Thus, maintaining ongoing communication at work is one element in helping everyone feel that his or her job is significant and the environment is comfortable.

➢ Some communication tools include:

✓ Directors Desk is a communication solution for boards.[2]

✓ Board Vantage is an online hosted service for confidential collaboration. Board Vantage supports the management of board communications and facilitates confidential collaboration among members of any group, including executive teams, deal teams, litigation teams, physician teams, and others.[3]

✓ iDashboards provide enterprise dashboard software.[4]

ENDNOTES

1. Prahalad and Hamel (1990).
2. See http://www.directorsdesk.com for more information.
3. See http://www.boardvantage.com for more information.
4. See http://www.idashboards.com for more information.

REFERENCES

Prahalad, C., Hamel, G. (1990). The core competence of the corporation, *Harvard Business Review*, 63(3), 79–91.

Chapter Eighteen
Corporate Governance Institutes and Networks

> The subjects covered in the Corporate Governance Institutes and Networks chapter include Social Exchange Theory (SET), Governance Network Theory (GNT) and Governance Networks and Professional Associations.

A corporation can be characterized as a collection of interdependent organizational functional units (divisions and departments) with formal and informal networks of relationships to form a complex system. Social exchange theory (SET) helps to provide insight into the nature of social networks as well as rationale behind the role that a social network plays within an organization. Researchers suggest that an employee's social network characteristics and capturing his or her structural position in the peer network.[1]

A board director should become aware of various corporate governance institutes and networks to help gauge the effectiveness of the board as well as his or her responsibility for effectively governing by fulfilling the duties of the governance position.

Social Exchange Theory (SET)
➢ Behavioral based theory.
➢ Explains knowledge sharing behavior - individuals interact with others based on a self-interested analysis of the costs and benefits.
➢ Maximize their benefits and minimize their costs.
➢ These benefits need not be tangible.
➢ People help others with an expectation of future return.
➢ Framework for analyzing organizations and understanding governance.[2]
➢ Researcher use Social exchange theory (SET) to support governance network theory (GNT).[3]

Without self-regulation, either the government or an industry will impose regulation. The real opportunity for self-regulation lies in each company's board of directors. They can examine the impact a board director's effectiveness in leadership and decision-making skills in the governance and wealth maximization for the company's shareholder. However, there are many corporate governance institutes and networks that can help boards with determining where to place effort for effective governances (refer to figure 19).

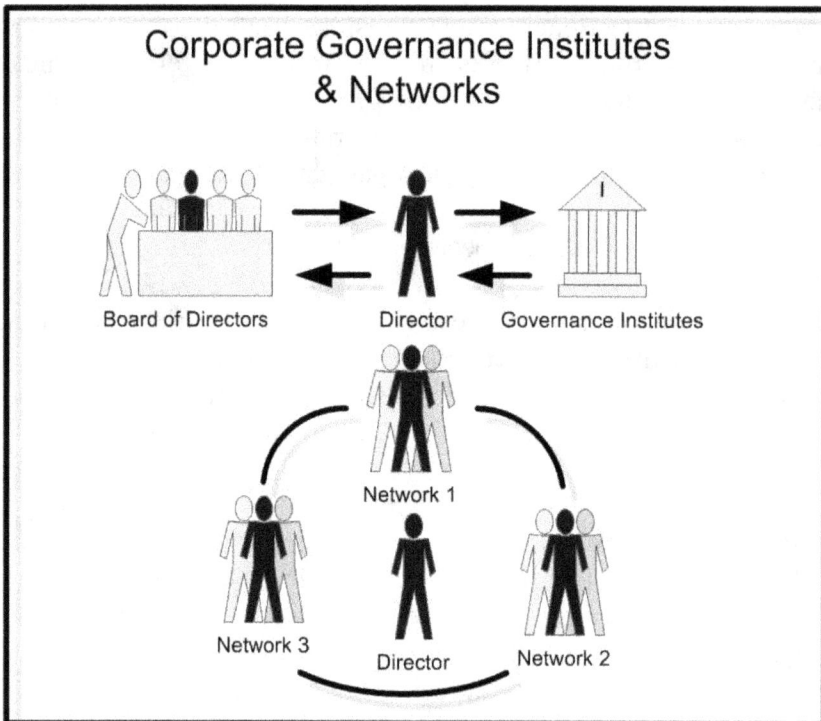

Figure 19 - Corporate Governance Institutes

Governance Network Theory (GNT)
➢ Network based theory.
➢ A phenomenon of the last thirty years.
➢ Deals with governance interactions, impact of institutional factors and management strategies. [4]
➢ Strategic actions occur during a strategizing process and generate governance networks.[5]
➢ Gained prominence within public administration.[6]

Governance Networks and Professional Associations

➢ The Board of Directors Network, Inc. is an organization of women and men representing boards of directors, corporations, government agencies, academia, legal and financial professions, nonprofit organizations, and media seeking to influence public companies to further the advancement of women in the boardroom and executive suites. This organization advocates for more women in both executive leadership and on corporate boards to improve corporate governance through diversity.[7]

➢ Institute of Directors is a worldwide association of members that provides a professional business community.[8]

➢ Board Source increases the effectiveness of nonprofit organizations by strengthening boards of directors through their highly acclaimed consulting practice, publications, tools, and membership program.[9]

➢ The Governance Institute is driven by its vision for health care, its hospital and health system clientele, and its own culture.[10]

➢ National Association of Corporate Directors is a national non-profit membership organization dedicated exclusively to serving the corporate governance needs of corporate boards and individual board members.[11]

➢ The International Corporate Governance Network is a global membership organization of around 450 leaders in corporate governance based in 45 countries with a mission to raise standards of corporate governance worldwide.[12]

➢ The Society of Corporate Secretaries and Governance Professionals, Inc. has over 3,800 members representing approximately 2,600 companies.[13]

ENDNOTES

1. Jussila, Goel, Tuominen (2012).
2. Sykes et al. (2009).
3. Newig, Gunther, Pahl-Wostl (2010).
4. Keast, Mandell, Agranoff (2013).
5. Montenegro & Bulgacov (2014).
6. Klijn, Koppenjan (2012).
7. See http://www.directorsnetwork.com/ for more information.
8. See http://www.iod.com for more information.
9. See http://www.boardsource.org for more information.
10. See http://www.governanceinstitute.com for more information.
11. See http://www.nacdonline.org for more information.
12. See http://www.icgn.org for more information.
13. See http://www.governanceprofessionals.org for more information.

REFERENCES

Jussila, I., Goel, S., Tuominen, P. (2012). Governance of co-operative organizations: a social exchange perspective, *Business Management Research*, 1(2), 14-24.

Keast, R., Mandell, M., Agranoff, R. (2013). *Network theory in the public sector: building new theoretical frameworks*, New York: Routledge.

Klijn, E. Koppenjan, J. (2012). Governance network theory: past, present and future, *Policy & Politics*, 40(4), 587-606.

Montenegro, L. M., Bulgacov, S. (2014). Reflections on actor-network theory, governance networks, and strategic outcomes. *Brazilian Administration Review*, 11(1), 107-124.

Newig, J., D. Günther, and C. Pahl-Wostl. (2010). Synapses in the network: learning in governance networks in the context of environmental management, *Ecology and Society*, 15(4), 24.

Sykes, T., Venkatesh, V., Gosain, S. (2009). Model of acceptance with peer support: A social network perspective to understand employees' system use, *MIS Quarterly*, 33(2), 371-393.

Part III
Governance Trends and Globalization

Chapter Nineteen
Emerging Governance Trends

> The subjects covered in the Emerging Governance Trends chapter include Information Security Governance, Embracing Information Security Complexity, Evangelizing an Information Security Culture, Chief Information Security Officer (CISO), Enhanced Board Transparency, Information Security Governance Framework, Prominence of a Chief Information Security Officer, Greater Proxy Access, Transparency with Succession Planning, and Greater Awareness of the Whistleblower Bounty Program.

A board director should become aware of emerging trends in governance in order to better his or her governance effectiveness associated with fulfilling the duties of the board director position. This is especially true in the areas including information security governance, proxy access, succession planning, whistle-blowing and brings a whole host of changes in responsibilities.

Information Security Governance
➤ In an ever changing world, information security practitioners are confronted with an increasing complexity in information security. An information security governance framework consists of security components and activities.
➤ Security leaders of an enterprise use the framework to support security strategies, program objectives and key program activities.
➤ A security professional can use the InfoSEC governance framework to help in providing an enterprise-wide view of governance and the establishment of appropriate, cost-effective information security governance programs.
➤ Within the context of a security governance framework, a security professional can better identify and perform activities that are strategic, managerial, operational, and/or technical.

Embracing Information Security Complexity

➤ Complexity comes in the form of governance and technology considerations combined with a security professional understanding of how to select relevant security controls and requirements from a diverse set of information security standards and guidelines.

Evangelizing an Information Security Culture

➤ In any size of organization or government agency there can be found an information security culture

➤ The health of the security culture can be good or bad depending on perceptions and exhibited behavior of the employees, suppliers and vendors

➤ The information security culture develops, grows and evolves within a particular organizational entity due to certain actions taken by individuals within the organization.

➤ An organizational leader such as the Chief Information Security Officer (CISO) establishes the strategic vision but management implements information security components, such as polices and technical security measures and procedures, and all employees that must follow the established security procedures.[1]

➤ To this end, employees develop certain perceptions and exhibit behavior, such as the reporting of security incidents or sharing of passwords, which could either contribute or pose as a threat to the security of information assets of the organization.

Information Security Governance Framework

➤ An information security governance framework consists of security components used by leaders, management and practitioners either in an organization or governmental agency to ensure that leadership is governing information security from a holistic perspective and in turn security management is minimizing risk and cultivating an acceptable level of information security culture demonstrated by all of the employees (e.g. Jericho Security and Risk Management Framework found within the reference model from Cloud Security Alliance[2] and the NIST Cloud Computing Security Reference Architecture[3]).

- Strategic Activities: Strategic Security Goals, Program Objectives and Key Program Activities.
  - ✓ Strategic Security Goals.

    - ❖ An example goal is ensuring the security and reliability of information systems.

  - ✓ Security Program Objectives

    - ❖ An example of a program objective is to protect information assets and people by minimizing risk exposure and by maximizing security through the implementation and monitoring of a comprehensive set of controls.

  - ✓ Key Security Program Activities

    - ❖ By nature key security program activities fall into one of the following activity sets: strategic, managerial and operational and technical.

    - ❖ Goals are supported by objectives where the objectives are carried out by key activities.

Prominence of a Chief Information Security Officer (CISO)
The CISO has both a role and responsibility within a particular organization.

- CISO Role

  - ✓ A CISO is responsible for the organization's entire security posture, both physical and digital.
  - ✓ The CISO frequently owns or participates closely in related areas such as business continuity planning, loss prevention and fraud prevention, and privacy.

➢   CISO Responsibility

✓ Oversee a network of security directors and vendors who safeguard the company's assets, intellectual property and computer systems, as well as the physical safety of employees and visitors.
✓ Identify protection goals, objectives and metrics consistent with a corporate strategic plan.
✓ Manage the development and implementation of global security policies, standards, guidelines and procedures to ensure ongoing maintenance of security.

❖ Physical protection responsibilities will include asset protection, workplace violence prevention, access control systems, video surveillance and more. Information protection responsibilities will include network security architecture, network access and monitoring policies and employee education and awareness.

✓ Work with other executives to prioritize security initiatives and spending based on appropriate risk management and/or financial methodology.
✓ Maintain relationships with local, state and federal law enforcement and other related government agencies.
✓ Oversee incident response planning as well as the investigation of security breaches, and assist with disciplinary and legal matters associated with such breaches as necessary.
✓ Work with outside consultants as appropriate for independent security audits.

Greater Proxy Access
➢ Proxy access (private ordering) is permitted on a company-by-company basis.
➢ Proxy access enables shareholders to nominate their own director candidates that can go up against those directors nominated by the company.

➤ Shareholders with at least $2,000 in a particular company's stock that has been held for at least one year are allowed to submit a proposal to amend the company bylaws to allow for direct proxy access.

 ✓ Once approved, a shareholder can submit his or her director to the director slate and include a director within the proxy statement the following year.

➤ Proactive outreach to large shareholders especially on vital issues is essential to avoiding director slate issues.

Transparency with Succession Planning

➤ Identifying and grooming potential candidates for CEO continues to be of major importance to directors.
➤ Increased scrutiny will continue to an issue, especially on the independence aspects of board leadership.
➤ In many directors' eyes the emphasis on strategic planning is a key activity going forward.

Greater Awareness of the Whistleblower Bounty Program

➤ SEC, authorized by Congress, to provide monetary rewards to whistleblowers.[4]
➤ Minimize harm to investors.
➤ Better preserve the integrity of the United States capital markets.
➤ Swiftly hold accountable those responsible for unlawful conduct.

ENDNOTES

1. Whitten (2008).
2. See http://cloudsecurityalliance.org for more information.
3. See http://collaborate.nist.gov/twiki-cloud-computing/pub/CloudComputing/CloudSecurity for more information
4. See http://www.sec.gov/whistleblower for more information.

REFERENCES

Whitten, D. (2008). The chief information officer: An analysis of skills required for success. *Journal of Computer Information Systems*, 48(3).

Chapter Twenty
Global Governance Comparison

The subjects covered in the Global Governance Comparison chapter include Global Standards in Governance, Global Governance Divergence, German Governance, and Family Owned Governance.

A board director should become aware of other governance practices outside of those practices used within the United States. A board director might find himself or herself on an international board. He or she might need to understand a different governance perspective associated with fulfilling the duties of the governance position. This chapter does not cover international members of American boards or American members of international boards.

In American business law, the board is the corporation's ultimate authority. As Drucker suggested more than three decades ago, board of directors will someday be declared redundant when these same boards of directors fail to respond regulators and legislators.[1] However, a potential risk is that, with most companies, existing board directors, advised by management, control the board nomination process, whereby the company's shareholders have little or no input.[2]

Global Standards in Governance
- Corporate governance practices are driven by both context and ownership structure found within a particular country so finding a global standard on corporate governance continues to be illusive.[3]
- Cultural factors in addition to economic factors influence corporate governance within a particular country.[4]

Global Governance Divergence
- Researchers have found greater divergence governance exists around the world.[5]
- Corporate governance varies from country to country.
- Governance practices in other countries do not necessarily follow corporate governance practices in the United States.

➢ Researchers observed that differences in business and cultural practices are necessary for companies operating in different countries.[6]

➢ By increasing shareholder value at the expense of other tangible needs is an American and other Western-based perspective and does not necessary transfer to non-Western cultures.[7]

United Kingdom Governance

➢ Researchers found that a UK company's financial characteristics such as size, profitability and leverage can influence corporate governance ratings from RiskMetrics/ISS.[8]

German Governance

➢ In German corporate governance, a Vorstand is the management board of a corporation where the Aufsichtsrat, or supervisory board, controls the Vorstand.

➢ On average, board members for a German company are older, have longer tenure, were less likely to have specific industry experience and were far less likely to be foreign other than in Europe's other big economies.[9]

➢ German supervisory boards are also often unwieldy, with up to 20 members. When the company's management is included, meetings can run to 30 people.

Family Owned Governance

➢ Many German companies are family-controlled with a focus on the relationship between minority and controlling shareholders, rather than on the control that shareholders as a whole exercise over managers.[10]

➢ Japan, China, and South Korea have dramatically different corporate governance models than the United States, United Kingdom, and Australia.[11]

➢ Researchers observed that, in most East Asian countries, family-owned companies dominate. The top fifteen families controlled more than half of publicly owned corporations through a system of family cross-holdings, thus dominating the capital markets.[12]

> ➤ Likewise, in the Latin model of corporate governance, family-owned companies dominated the list in Italy, Mexico, Spain, Brazil, Argentina, and other countries in South America. The same is true to a certain extent in France.

ENDNOTES

1. Park (2013).
2. See "Time to boot celebrities, enact board reforms" (2005).
3. Bebchuk and Hamdani (2009).
4. Chan and Cheung (2012).
5. Guillen (2001); Hollingsworth (1997); Khanna et al. (2003); Whitley (1999).
6. Fish (1999).
7. Jackson (2002).
8. Carcello and Neal (2003).
9. See "Boards behaving badly" (2009).
10. See "Boards behaving badly" (2009).
11. Holstein (2006).
12. Claessens, Djankov and Lang (2000).

REFERENCES

Bebchuk, L.A., Hamdani, A. (2009), *The elusive quest for global governance standards*, University of Pennsylvania Law Review, 157(5), pp. 1263-317.

"Boards behaving badly" (2009). *The Economist*, August 6, 2009.

Chan, A., Cheung , H. (2012). Cultural dimensions, ethical sensitivity, and corporate governance, *Journal of Business Ethics*, 110(45), 59.

Carcello, J., & Neal, T. (2003). Audit committee independence and disclosure: Choice for financial distressed firms. *Corporate Governance: An International Review*, 11(4), 289–299.

Claessens, S., Djankov, S., Fan, J. P., & Lang, L. H. (2002). Disentangling the incentive and entrenchment effects of large shareholdings. *The Journal of Finance*, *57*(6), 2741-2771.

Fish, A. (1999) Cultural diversity: Challenges facing the management of cross-board business careers, *Career Development International*, 4(4), 196-205.

Guillen, M. F. (2001). *The limits of convergence: Globalization and organizational change in Argentina, Korea and Spain.* Princeton, NJ: Princeton University Press.

Hollingsworth, J. R. (1997). Continuities and changes in social systems of production: The cases of Japan, Germany and the United States. In R. Boyer & J. R. Hollingsworth (Eds.), *Contemporary capitalism: The embeddedness of* institutions (pp. 260–282). Cambridge, MA: Cambridge University Press.

Jackson, T. (2002). The management of people across cultures: Valuing people differently, *Human Resource Management,* 41(4), 455-476.

Khanna, T., Kogan, J., & Palepu, K. (2003). Globalization and similarities in corporate governance: A cross-country analysis. *Review of Economics and Statistics,* 88(1), 69–90.

Holstein, W. (2006). GMI rates governance by country. *Directorship* 11.

Park, M. (2013). The economic meltdown -- a morality tale. *Keeping Good Companies (14447614), 65*(1), 31-35.

"Time to boot celebrities, enact board reforms" (2005). *Crain's Chicago Business,* November 28, 2005.

Whitley, R. D. (Ed.). (1999). *Divergent capitalisms: The social structuring and change of business systems.* Oxford: Oxford University Press.

Conclusion

The conclusions drawn from the analysis of relevant literature that is publicly available presents a broad foundation in support of covering the various aspects of corporate governance. The literature reviewed the historical and recent popular aspects of the characteristics of individual board directors, identifying any common patterns to suggest the collective balance of a board director and whether a board enhances or impairs corporate governance on behalf of the shareholder.

The *Pocket Guide* provides new knowledge in understanding a unique aspect of what it means to be a board director. Holding directorship status, from the shareholder perspective, for a member of a company's board of directors is of interest due to potential impact on leadership effectiveness, corporate governance, and wealth maximization of the company's shareholders.

Even though it is not possible to turn back the clock with the events that have occurred over the last few years, includes failures in various boardrooms, shareholders have focused greater attention on corporate leadership and governance. Each year, the board of director's position becomes more complicated because there are more legal, due diligence, requirements from the Sarbanes-Oxley Act of 2002. Board directors that do not take action now by taking time to educate themselves with the latest information on corporate governance might find themselves ill prepared for the task at hand; especially, as class action lawsuits continue to become common place.

The *Pocket Guide* was not simply written for the active board director. *Pocket Guide* was written for shareholders, investors, instructors, students, governance practitioners, lawyers, international readers, and anyone interested in corporate governance.

Dr. Eric Yocam has accumulated over 22 year experience in industry. As a researcher, his research interests are in the areas of corporate governance, leadership, real option theory and fuzzy logic.

His governance experience includes participation on both for-profit and non-profit organizations. He was Vice-Chair of the Governing Board of Directors for the Northwest Dollars for Scholars (NWDS) non-profit organization located in Bellevue, WA. Northwest Dollars for Scholars is a program of Scholarship America, with headquarters based in MN, the nation's largest private sector scholarship and educational support organization. Yocam was also the Managing Director on the Board of Directors for Yocam Holdings LLC for a number of years. Yocam Holdings LLC was a privately held for-profit investment corporation.

He holds a doctor of business administration degree (DBA) from the School of Advanced Studies at the University of Phoenix, a master of science degree in computer science from the College of Engineering, Computer Science and Technology at California State University-Chico, a master of science degree in finance from the Albers School of Business and Economics at Seattle University, a master of business administration degree from the School of Business Administration at the University of San Diego, and a bachelor of science degree in computer engineering from the School of Engineering at the University of the Pacific.

Dr. Siu Kuen Annie Choi is a licensed attorney in the state of Washington. As a legal researcher, her research interests are in the areas of corporate governance, international business, and immigration law.

She holds a Juris Doctor from Thomas Jefferson School of Law in San Diego, California; a master of international business degree from the School of Business Administration at the University of San Diego in San Diego, California; and a bachelor of business administration from the School of Business Administration at the University of San Diego in San Diego, California.

Send Us Feedback

Any and all feedback is welcome. The authors want to ensure that this publication stays current and remains an authoritative source on corporate governance. To this end, the authors encourage the reader's feedback on any subject found within this publication.

The authors would like readers' input for inclusion of additional key subjects and other important information that should be part of this publication.

E-mail feedback about this publication to
eric.yocam@yocampublishing.biz

Yocam Publishing LLC

Information about upcoming publications by the authors of this work can be found at *http://www.yocampublishing.biz*

Yocam Publishing LLC is a company committed to promoting awareness on various contemporary subjects of interest, enriching professional best practice and encouraging practical application from new findings of theoretical research.

The board of director position is becoming harder, and the board director must spend a significant amount of effort to keep abreast of changes in corporate governance.

In order to encourage and promote awareness and best practices, the board director should invest any available time through self-education and subscribing to periodicals on corporate governance. A board director should become aware of various corporate governance periodicals and online resources to help with keeping abreast of changes in governance associated with fulfilling the duties of the governance position.

Business Ethics
(http://www.business-ethics.com) reports on the fields of business ethics and corporate governance, tracking major regulatory changes and their impact on corporate behavior. It also examines the broader social role of companies and their accountability to multiple stakeholders – shareholders, employees, customers and the communities where companies do business.

Business Roundtable
(http://www.businessroundtable.org) is an association of chief executive officers of leading U.S. companies with more than $5 trillion in annual revenues and more than 10 million employees. Member companies comprise nearly a third of the total value of the U.S. stock markets and pay nearly half of all corporate income taxes paid to the federal government.

Board Seat Search Company (Lightship Employment Solutions)
(http://www.lightshipemploymentsolutions.com) is a company that specializes in matching director candidates with a board seat. There are approximately 60,000 publicly traded companies and an additional 20,000 private companies with boards of directors in the United States. This results in a total of 80,000 boards nationwide. Experts estimate that the average board tenure lasts approximately eight years, meaning that in any given year, up to 10,000 board seats must be filled.

Compensation Standards
(http://www.compensationstandards.com) is a "one stop" resource for information about responsible executive compensation practices.

Corporate Governance
(http://corpgov.net) was founded in 1995 to provide news, commentary and a network on the subject of corporate governance.

Directors and Boards Magazine
(http://www.directorsandboards.com) has provided thought leadership in corporate governance since 1976.

Directorship
(http://www.directorship.com) delivers the most comprehensive intelligence and research on leading-edge practices in corporate governance and boardroom decision-making.

Investor Relations Magazine
Investor Relations Magazine (http://www.thecrossbordergroup.com) delivers the most comprehensive intelligence and research on leading-edge practices in corporate governance and boardroom decision-making.

National Investor Relations Institute
(http://www.niri.org) was founded in 1969, NIRI is the professional association of corporate officers and investor relations consultants responsible for communication among corporate management, shareholders, securities analysts and other financial community constituents. NIRI is the largest professional investor relations association in the world.

The Conference Board
(http://www.conference-board.org) has created and disseminated knowledge about management and the marketplace to help businesses strengthen their performance and better serve society.

The Corporate Board
(http://www.corporateboard.com) is the nation's leading corporate governance magazine, providing corporate directors and senior executive officers with information vital to the efficiency and success of their corporate governance actions.

The Corporate Counsel
(http://www.thecorporatecounsel.net) is an educational service that provides practical guidance on legal issues involving corporate and securities regulation and corporate governance practices - as well as many other areas impacting today's corporate practitioner.

Shareholder Communications Coalition
(http://www.shareholdercoalition.com) is actively working in Congress to build support for a comprehensive review of the proxy rules by the U.S. Securities and Exchange Commission (SEC).

Society of Corporate Secretaries and Governance Professionals
(http://www.governanceprofessionals.org) was founded in 1946 as the American Society of Corporate Secretaries, has over 3,100 members representing approximately 2,500 companies. Its members deal with public disclosure under the securities laws and matters affecting corporate governance, including the structure and meetings of the board of directors and its committees, the proxy process and the annual meeting of shareholders and shareholder relations, particularly with large institutional owners.

GLOSSARY

A

Activist shareholder: The use of an equity stake in a corporation to put public pressure on the corporation's management. It can take any of several forms: proxy battles, publicity campaigns, shareholder resolutions, litigation, and negotiations with management.

Anti-takeover Provision: A defensive position taken by a company's incumbent board of directors. It includes poison pill adoptions and anti-takeover amendments, it is found within a company's corporate charter, in order to increase the bargaining power of a company's incumbent board of directors and restrict the acquirer from taking corporate control of the company.

Agency Theory: A process in which potentially a self-interested director appropriates value to himself, hence, conflict arises because the director is acting as an agent on behalf of the shareholder. Agency theory is about resolving two problems that can occur in agency relationships. For example, in the case of the director, a two agency problem exists. First, an agency problem occurs when the desires or goals of the shareholder and director are in conflict. Second, an agency problem occurs when oversight is both difficult and expensive for shareholders (verifying the actions of the director on the shareholders' behalf).

B

Balanced scorecard: The balanced scorecard, developed by Robert S. Kaplan and David P. Norton, is a coherent set of performance measures organized into four categories. It includes traditional financial measures, but adds customer, internal business process, and learning and growth perspectives. Refer to Business Balanced Scorecard.

Benchmarking: A systematic approach to comparing an organization's performance against peers and competitors in an effort to learn the best ways of conducting business.

Best Practice: A proven activity or process that has been successfully used by multiple organizations.

Blackout period: Refers to a temporary period in which access is limited or denied. Board director or executive officer purchasing, selling or otherwise acquiring or transferring securities is prohibited during blackout period.

Block holder: A representation of a controlling interest in a company. In other words, it is when one has control of a large enough block of voting stock shares in a company such that no one stockholder or coalition of stockholders can successfully oppose a motion.

Board of Directors: A group of professionals who bring breadth of skills, experience, and diversity to a company. It also refers to the directors collectively who are charged with the conduct and the management of a company.

Board of Directors Retreat (Offsite): A single or multi-day offsite meeting to discuss strategy, build stronger teams, formulate goals.

Board size: A count of people holding directorships participating on a board of directors.

Breach of Duty: An occurrence when the officer of the company, as a reasonable person, fails to execute the duties of his or her position as an agent for the company and on behalf of the shareholders.

Business Balanced Scorecard: A tool for managing organizational strategy which uses weighted measures for the areas of financial performance (lag) indicators,
internal operations, customer measurements, learning and growth (lead) indicators combined to rate the organization. Refer to Balanced Scorecard.

Business Case: Documentation of the rationale for making a business investment used both to support a business decision on whether to proceed or not with the investment and as an operational tool to support management of the investment through its full economic life cycle.

Business Intelligence: A set of skills, technologies, applications and practices used to help a business acquire a better understanding of its commercial context. Business intelligence may also refer to the collected information itself.

Business Judgment Rule: A good faith effort by the director to obtain information in order to avoid class action lawsuits by shareholders.

Business Process: An inter-related set of cross-functional activities or events that result in the delivery of a specific product or service to a customer.

Business Process Engineering: a technique to improve processes by looking at what already exists and deciding how to improve it.

Business Process Improvement: A systematic technique to help any organization make significant changes in the way it does business.

Buzzword Governance: The use of words that only have meaning to the people practicing and/or interested in the art of governance.

Business Process Reengineering (BPR): The thorough analysis and significant redesign of business processes and management systems to establish a better performing structure, more responsive to the customer base and market conditions, while yielding material cost savings.

Bylaws: Documentation containing detailed management provisions and rules binding to directors, officers, and shareholders.

C

Capability: An aptitude, competency or resource that an enterprise may possess or require at an enterprise, business function, or individual level that has the potential or/is required to contribute to a business outcome and to creating value.

C-Level Management: Describes high-ranking executive titles within an organization such as CEO (Chief Executive Officer).

Capability Maturity Model (CMM): Contains the essential elements of effective processes for one or more disciplines. It also describes an evolutionary improvement path from ad hoc, immature processes to disciplined, mature processes with improved quality and effectiveness.

Cause and Effect: A quality management technique created by Kaoru Ishikawa that uses diagrams to map the relationship between cause and effect.

Celebrity: A famous person or a person who is widely known both in society and business community who commands a degree of public and media attention. The celebrity possesses one or more traits including credibility, goodwill, rights, image, influence, liabilities, and standard of value.

Celebrity Board Director: An officer with significant influence in the company's governance decision making. He or she possesses one or more traits including credibility, goodwill, rights, image, influence, liabilities, and standard of value.

Celebrity Goodwill: A reflection of a number of factors including age, health, past earning power, reputation, skill, comparative success, and length of time in business.

Celebrity Valuation: A representation if the valuation techniques used to calculate the celebrity goodwill including income, market, and asset based.

Center of Excellence (COE): A particular organizational structure that represents either a formally or informally accepted centralized body of knowledge and experience on a particular subject area.

Change Management: A holistic and proactive approach to managing the transition from a current to a desired organizational state, focusing specifically on the critical human or "soft" elements of change.

Chairman of the Board of Directors: A person who leads the board of directors.

Chief Executive Officer (CEO): Chief executive officer is the highest ranking individual in an organization.

Chief Financial Officer (CFO): Chief financial officer is the individual primarily responsible for managing the financial risks of an organization.

Chief Information Security Officer (CISO): Chief information security officer is the individual primarily responsible for managing the information security risks of an organization.

Chief Technology Officer (CTO): The individual who focuses on technical issues in an organization.

Classified Board of Directors: A practice of governing in which the members of the board of directors are elected a few at a time, with different groups of directors having overlapping multi-year terms, instead of en masse (where all directors have one-year terms).Each group of directors falls within a specified "class"—e.g., Class I, Class II, etc.—hence the use of the term "classified" board. **See Staggered Board of Directors.**

Cloud Computing: A type of computing relying on shared computing resources instead of having dedicated local servers or personal devices to handle software applications.

COBIT: The Control Objectives for Information and related Technology (CoBiT) from ISACA is a set of best practices for IT management. CoBiT focuses on defining program and management control functions. It is designed to help ensure IT programs are implemented and managed effectively to maximize the investment of technology efficiently.

Committee: A collection of directors for a specific purpose, for example, to manage finances or human resources. Many different types of committees are organized for various purposes.

Community of Practice (CoP): Groups of people performing similar roles that interact based on common needs and concerns to share and increase knowledge.

Competencies: The strengths of an organization, what it does well.

Contingency Planning: Process of developing advance arrangements and procedures that enable an organization to respond to an event that could occur by chance or unforeseen circumstances.

Continuous Improvement: The goals of continuous improvement (Kaizen) include the elimination of waste, defined as "activities that add cost but do not add value;" just-in-time delivery; production load leveling of amounts and types; standardized work; paced moving lines; right-sized equipment.

Corporate Governance: The set of processes, customs, policies, laws, and institutions affecting the way a corporate is directed, administered, or controlled.

Corporate Information Security Officer (CISO): Responsible for coordinating the planning, development, implementation, maintenance and monitoring of the information security program.

COSO: The Committee of Sponsoring Organizations of the Treadway Commission defined the Control Objectives for their Internal Control – Integrated Framework, the widely accepted control framework for enterprise governance and risk management, and similar compliant framework and was established 1985. COSO defines a set of business, management, and security relevant controls that can be used to demonstrate good business practice controls, and can be used to show compliance with Sarbanes Oxley requirements.

Critical Success Factors (CSFs): Critical success factor; the most important issues or actions for management to achieve control over and within its IT processes.

D

Delegated voting: See **Proxy voting.**

Digital Dashboard: A business management tool used to visually ascertain the status or "health" of a business enterprise via key business indicators.

Director: An officer of the company charged with the conduct and management of its affairs. A director may be an inside director or an outside director.

Disaster Recovery: Activities and programs designed to return the organization to an acceptable condition. The ability to respond to an interruption in services by implementing a disaster recovery plan to restore an organization's critical business functions.

Dissident Shareholder: A dissident shareholder is a person who opposes a corporation's management or management policy. For example, dissident shareholders of Hewlett-Packard opposed that corporation's offer to purchase Compaq Computer. See **Activist shareholder.**

Dodd-Frank Wall Street Reform and Consumer Protection Act: This acts key provisions include consumer and investor protection, executive compensation Say on pay vote once every 3 years by shareholders, corporate governance proxy access, and reason for same person as both Chair and CEO.

Domain Knowledge: A representation of a person's accumulation of expertise in a particular subject areas based on his or her experience, education, and skills.

Duality with Chairman/CEO Position: A representation of a situation when a single person holds two positions at a company as both the chairman of the board and CEO.

Due Diligence: The performance of those actions that are generally regarded as prudent, responsible and necessary to conduct a thorough and objective investigation, review and/or analysis.

Duty of Obedience: An occurrence when a director must obey the law and regulations giving him or her authority to manage a corporation.

Duty of Care: An occurrence when a director must use prudent judgment and act with ordinary good faith in self-judgment.

Duty of Loyalty: An occurrences when a director must put his or her personal interests after the corporate interest.

E

Enterprise Dashboard: See Digital Dashboard.

Ethics: The study of morality or moral standards (Velasquez 1998). Ethics are a sort of guideline that is used daily to motivate a person to do the right thing (McAdams, Freeman, and Pincus 1995).

Executive Dashboard: See Digital Dashboard.

Executive Director: A person who is a senior manager or executive officer of an organization, company, or corporation.

F

FISMA from NIST: The Federal Information Security Management Act, also known as FISMA is a U.S. federal law enacted in 2002. FISMA is to improve computer and network security within the Federal Government. It also applies to government contractors. These processes must follow a combination of Federal Information Processing standards (FIPS) documents, the special publications SP-800 series issued by NIST, and other legislation pertinent to federal information systems, such as the Privacy Act of 1974 and the Health Insurance Portability and Accountability Act.

Financial Accounting Standards Board (FASB): A private, not-for-profit organization whose primary purpose is to develop generally accepted accounting principles (GAAP) within the United States in the public's interest.

Fair Market Value: A representation of the amount paid for a product or service when compared to other comparable products or services by a number of buyers.

Fiduciary duty: A legal or ethical relationship of confidence or trust between two or more parties, most commonly a fiduciary or trustee and a principal or beneficiary.

Five Whys: A technique using questions to explore the cause and effect relationships underlying a particular problem.

For-profit Corporation: A corporation that is intended to operate a business that will return a profit to the owners.

G

Generally accepted accounting principles (GAAP): See **Financial Accounting Standards Board (FASB).**

Governance Index (G-index): Twenty-four governance provisions that have been classified into five categories of management power. A higher G-index indicates lower shareholder rights and weaker governance.

Globalization: The development from increasing global connectivity, integration, and interdependence in economic, social, technological, cultural, political, and ecological spheres.

Governance Score (G-score): Fifty-one factors representing either one or zero, depending on whether the company's governance standards are acceptable or unacceptable.

Governance: A leadership process supporting decisions that define expectations, grant power, or verify performance.

Governance Network: The interaction of individuals who represent boards of directors, corporations, government agencies, academia, the legal and financial professions, and nonprofit organizations.

Governance Metrics International: An organization dedicated to monitoring and rating corporations worldwide on several governance points. The goal of this organization is to provide an easy-to-use tool to show investors and other interested parties how effective the governance practices of a particular corporation are.

Governance Type: Refers to the type of company a person is governing, for example, nonprofit (not-for-profit) or for profit.

H

Health Insurance Portability and Accountability Act (HIPAA): A law establishing national standards for electronic health care transactions and national identifiers for providers, health plans, and employers. It also addressed the security and privacy of health data.

I

Independent Director: See **Non-executive Director**.

Inside Director: A director who is also an officer.

Intellectual capital: Resources that determine the value and the competitiveness of a company. See Knowledge Asset.

Interconnected board: A situation when two or more directors that are sitting on multiple boards.

Interlocked board: Occurs when two boards have a CEO from the other company sitting on the board of company.

Investment Value: A representation of the amount a standard of value for celebrity goodwill.

ISMS: A set of policies concerned with information security management or IT related risks.

ISO 27001: Specifies a management system that is intended to bring information security under explicit management control. Being a formal specification means that it mandates specific requirements.

ISO 27002: Provides best practice recommendations on information security management for use by those responsible for initiating, implementing or maintaining ISMS

ITIL: A set of concepts and practices for Information Technology Services Management (ITSM), Information Technology (IT) development and IT operations.

K

Key Performance Indicators (KPIs): Financial and non-financial metrics that quantify objectives to reflect strategic performance of an organization.

Knowledge Asset: Company-specific resource that is indispensable to create value for a company. They are the inputs, outputs, and moderating factors, of the knowledge-creating process.

L

Law: A broad and important principle. See **Principle**.

Leadership: The ability to influence, motivate, and enable others to contribute toward the effectiveness of the organizations of which they are members.

M

Mentoring board members: A board mentorship program is about building governing skills, establishing governing programs and measuring program effectiveness in order to ensure a right fit for a governance board. No one size fits all approach. Mentoring requires leadership, knowledge, skill, experience, courage, and patience.

Mergers and Acquisition: An aspect of corporate strategy, corporate finance and management dealing with the buying, selling and combining of different companies that can aid, finance, or help a growing company in a given industry grow rapidly without having to create another business entity.

Mergers and Acquisition Market: No actual marketplace currently exists. The process by which a company is bought or sold can prove difficult, slow and expensive. A transaction typically lengthy and involves many steps. An industry of professional "middlemen" (known

variously as intermediaries, business brokers, and investment bankers) exists to facilitate transactions.

Morality: The study of standards for either an individual or a group

Majority voting: A "majority" voting standard for director elections when the company's governing documents provide that directors must receive support from holders of a majority of shares voted in order to be considered legally elected.

N

Non-executive director: A member of the board of directors of a company who does not form part of the executive management team.

Nonprofit Corporation (also called a not-for-profit corporation): An entity that is usually created with a specific purpose, for example, educational, charitable, or other enumerated purpose. It may be a foundation, charity or other type of similar organization.

O

Off balance sheet (OBS): an asset or debt or financing activity not on the company's balance sheet.

Outside director: See Non-executive Director.

Options backdating: A practice of granting an employee stock option that is dated prior to the date that the company actually granted the option.

P

Performance Indicators: A set of metrics designed to measure the extent to which performance objectives are being achieved on an on-going basis.

Performance Management: In IT, the ability to manage any type of measurement including employee, team, and process, operational or financial measurements. The term connotes closed-loop control and regular monitoring of the measurement.

Poor governance: An occurrence when the board of directors did not live up to the expectation of a company's stakeholders.

Poison pill: An anti-takeover provision to force a would-be company acquirer to negotiate with the target takeover company's board of directors.

Portfolio: A grouping of "objects of interest" (investment programs, IT services, IT projects, other IT assets or resources) managed and monitored to optimize business value. (The investment portfolio is of primary interest to Val IT. T service, project, asset and other resource portfolios are of primary interest to COBIT).

Program: A structured grouping of interdependent projects that is both necessary and sufficient to achieve a desired business outcome and create value. These projects could include, but not be limited to, changes in the nature of the business, business processes, the work performed by people, as well as the competencies required to carry out the work, enabling technology, and organizational structure.

Project: A structured set of activities concerned with delivering a defined capability (that is necessary but not sufficient to achieve a required business outcome) to the enterprise based on an agreed-upon schedule and budget.

Project Portfolio: The set of projects owned by a company.

Principle: A useful generalization.

Private Investment in Public Equity (PIPE): A financing technique is popular due to the relative efficiency in time and cost of PIPEs, compared to more traditional forms of financing such as secondary offerings.

Professionalism: A person's ability to demonstrate courtesy, honesty, and responsibility in one's dealings with customers and associates in addition to a level of excellence that goes over and above the commercial considerations and legal requirements.

Proxy fight: A proxy fight or proxy battle is an event that may occur when a corporation's stockholders develop opposition to some aspect of the corporate governance, often focusing on directorial and management positions. Activist shareholders may attempt to persuade other shareholders to use their proxy votes. For example, an activist shareholder wants to get votes by one individual or institution as the authorized representative of another in order to install new management for any of a variety of reasons.

Proxy Voting: A procedure for the delegation to another member of a voting body of that member's power to vote in his or her absence.

Public corporation: A legal entity permitted to offer securities for sale to the public.

Privately held corporation: A company owned by one or more company founders or possibly their families or heirs or by a small group of investors.

R

RACI Chart: Illustrates who is responsible, accountable, consulted and informed within an organizational framework.

Remuneration: A monetary payment for services rendered.

Retreat: See **Board of Directors Retreat**.

Riddick's Rules of Procedure: A manual on parliamentary procedure for common usage for civic clubs and organizations. See **Robert's Rules of Order**.

Risk: The combination of the probability of an event and its consequence.

Risk Management: A human activity integrating the recognition of risk, risk assessment, developing strategies to manage it, and mitigation of risk using managerial resources.

Robert's Rules of Order: A book containing rules of order intended to be adopted for use by a deliberative assembly. See **Rules of Order**.

Rules of Order: Also known as standing orders or rules of procedure are the written rules of parliamentary procedure adopted by a deliberative assembly, which detail the processes used by the body to make decisions.

S

S439 of the Companies Act 2006: mandates a vote on board director pay at the yearly annual meeting.

Sarbanes-Oxley Act of 2002: A law enacted by the United States Congress and enforced by the Securities and Exchange Commission (SEC) to address financial stewardship concerns by shareholders with a company's leadership.

Say on pay: A term used for a rule in corporate law whereby a corporation's shareholders have the right to vote on the remuneration of directors.

Serial entrepreneur: A type of entrepreneur who starts a new business after having already started and exited a previous business venture.

Service Level Agreement: An agreement, preferably documented, between a service provider and the customer(s)/user(s) that defines minimum performance targets for a service and how they will be measured.

Shareholder Activism: A person who attempts to use his or her rights as a shareholder of a publicly-traded corporation to bring about social change.

Shareholder meeting: A type of gathering held with directors or management. It is usually held annually with all of the shareholders of a corporation electing the board of directors and hearing reports on the company's business performance.

Shareholder: A person with an ownership claim of the company where the claim is typically reflected in a company's share of common stock.

Shareholder wealth maximization: A representation of a shareholder's motive in gaining the maximum amount of economic value from appreciation of a company's share of common stock.

Situation decomposition: An analysis technique that uses the Strengths, Weakness, Opportunities, and Threats (SWOT) technique to gain a better understanding of the situation prior to making decisions.

Six-Sigma: A technique employed to systematically improve processes by eliminating defects.

Slate: A list of director nominees placed on the company ballot for election.

Social Responsibility: reflects the ethical rights and duties existing between a company and society.

Special Purpose Vehicle (SPV): A tax-exempt company or trust formed for the specific purpose of funding the assets and it is also known as a special purpose entity (SPE).

Staggered board of directors: A practice governing the board of directors of a company, corporation, or other organization in which the members of the board of directors are elected a few at a time, with different groups of directors having overlapping multi-year terms, instead of en masse (where all directors have one-year terms). See **Classified Board.**

Stakeholder Theory: The theory applied to corporate governance where multiple or competing interests represented by various interested parties for a particular company, including the board of directors, with an objective to receive some type of benefit.

Standard: A mandatory requirement, code of practice or specification approved by a recognized external standards organization, such as ISO.

Strategic Performance Management: The process where steering of the organization takes place through the systematic definition of mission, strategy and objectives of the organization, making these measurable through critical success factors and key performance

indicators, in order to take corrective actions necessary to keep the organization on track.

Strategic Planning: The process of deciding on the organization's objectives, on changes in these objectives, and the policies to govern their acquisition and use.

Strategy: A plan of action or policy designed toward achieving a major or overall aim.

Strengths, Weakness, Opportunities, and Threats (SWOT) Technique: A combination of an organizational audit listing the organization's strengths and weaknesses and an environmental scan or analysis of external opportunities and threats. Refer to Situation Decomposition.

Stewardship Theory: A theory applied to corporate governance where, as an agent on behalf of the stakeholder, a board director's motivation is to do a good job with managing corporate assets as a good steward.

Succession Planning: A plan to fill board vacancies before they occur.

Supervisory board: Corporate Governance varies among countries, especially regarding a board system. German corporation law requires all companies to have two boards: a management board and a supervisory board. The supervisory board is a group of individuals chosen by the stockholders of a company to promote their interests through the governance of the company and to hire and supervise the executive directors and CEO.

T

Taguchi Technique: A quality management technique developed by Genici Taguci, emphasizing minimizing variation as the main means of improving quality.

Total Cost of Ownership (TCO): A financial estimate technique to help consumers and managers assess costs related to any purchases.

Total Quality Management (TQM): A management technique aimed at embedding awareness of quality in all organizational processes.

V

Value: The relative worth or importance of an investment for an organization, as perceived by its key stakeholders, expressed as total life cycle benefits net of related costs, adjusted for risk and (in the case of financial value) the time value of money.

Virtue Ethics: A creation of the greatest good for all of the stakeholders.

W

Wealth: A representation of the economic value of an accumulation of intangible or tangible resources.

Wealth Maximization: A representation of gaining the maximum amount of economic value.

White-collar Crime: The result of a person acting in interest of company but commits a crime through his or her action.

White-label product: A white label product or service is a product or service produced by one company (the producer) that other companies (the marketers) rebrand to make it appear as if they made it.

Whistleblower: A person who identifies a law violation, misconduct, or fraud and reports it to authorities.

Index